mind & mood FOODS

mind & *mood* FOODS

OVER 100 DELICIOUS RECIPES TO BOOST YOUR BRAIN POWER, CALM YOUR MIND AND LIFT YOUR SPIRITS

HAZEL COURTENEY & KATHRYN MARSDEN

RECIPES CREATED BY ANNE SHEASBY

TED SMART

This edition produced for
THE BOOK PEOPLE LTD
Hall Wood Avenue, Haydock,
St Helens WA11 9UL

ISBN 1-85613-773-2

A CIP catalogue record for this book is available from the British Library

This book was designed and produced by
THE IVY PRESS LIMITED
The Old Candlemakers
West Street
Lewes, East Sussex
BN7 2NZ

Art Director: *Peter Bridgewater*
Editorial Director: *Sophie Collins*
Managing Editor: *Anne Townley*
Commissioning Editor: *Viv Croot*
Designer: *Clare Barber*
Project Editor: *Caroline Earle*
Editor: *Molly Perham*
Photography: *Marie-Louise Avery*

Printed and bound in China

'Food for thought – that is what this book is all about.'

HAZEL COURTENEY

foreword

Until I met my co-author, nutritionist Kathryn Marsden, 20 years ago it never occurred to me that my mood swings, constant tiredness, inability to concentrate and memory lapses were in any way related to my diet.

Millions of people suffer from similar symptoms, which are often blamed on age, lifestyle and even the weather. For the most part we accept these symptoms as being part of modern life and put up with them, believing that the way we feel most of the time is normal – but it is not. In Mind & Mood Foods, *Kathryn and I encourage you to take control of how you want to feel to suit your unique body and lifestyle. Food for thought – that is what this book is all about. It tells you which foods will help to feed your brain, improve memory and concentration, calm you down and lift your spirits. It is all a question of balance.*

Many people talk about healthy food, but in reality continue to eat poorly. Most people are unaware that our bodies are made up completely of molecules that we in some way derive from food – indeed, we are what we eat.

We realise that food alone cannot heal certain mental conditions that require medical attention. And we do not promise overnight miracles. But if you wish to become healthier and stay that way, by choosing this book you have already taken one step in the right direction. The rest is up to you.

Happy eating!

HAZEL COURTENEY

contents

introduction

The beans in these tacos provide protein, B vitamins and zinc – essential for healthy brain tissue and good memory function.

The secret to maintaining a healthy mind and body is to forget the word 'dieting' and think, instead, of introducing some balance and variety into every aspect of life. You have probably heard the phrase 'use it or lose it'. This is true for the whole body, but as we age it is especially important for us to keep our mind active. The average human brain contains ten billion nerve cells and weighs about 1.5kg (3lb). As the entire body, brain and nervous system is made of food molecules, our choice of food has an enormous effect on moods and brain function. In this book Kathryn and I have selected many nutritious foods to redress any imbalance in your diet using foods that heal rather than foods that harm. But don't panic – you can still enjoy your favourite treats. I'm sure you have heard the saying 'a little of what you fancy does you good' – but note the word little! When you eat something naughty, really enjoy it and don't feel guilty, but remember: balance in all things, and keep refined, sugary, fatty meals and treats to a minimum.

Today our bodies are bombarded by pollution, food additives, prescription drugs and chemicals, many of which did not exist 60 years ago, and when these accumulate within the body, our minds, moods and overall health are being affected. Alcohol, excessive refined sugar and processed foods can all 'fog' the brain causing a variety of symptoms, depending on the individual. We are all unique and this book will help you to find the right foods to suit how you want to feel.

Low blood sugar can cause poor memory and brain function. The secret to controlling blood sugar – and maybe your mood swings – is to eat well-balanced meals and healthy snacks at regular intervals and to make sure you eat breakfast. Above all, reduce the amount of refined sugar you eat and drink; mass-produced foods and drinks have little nutritional value and when eaten in excess replace other wholesome foods in the diet and thus can deplete the body of vital nutrients. Allergy sufferers are painfully aware of how eating the wrong foods can affect their health, but we all need to remember that the right food is like a medicine, and that a balanced diet is one of the simplest ways to better health.

To survive, the human body and brain need many nutrients including vitamins, minerals, amino acids and essential fatty acids, plus air, water and light. Our bodies cannot manufacture many of these nutrients; we must obtain them from external sources. For good health we need to eat sufficient quantities of high quality, fresh, unrefined whole foods. Because many fruits and vegetables are flown thousands of kilometres to reach our table and, once harvested, can lose up to 50 per cent of their vitamin content in just 10 days, we recommend that you eat locally grown, seasonal, preferably organic foods whenever possible.

Vitamins, minerals, amino acids and essential fats from our food work synergistically (together) within the body, so you derive greater benefits from eating a variety of whole foods, rather than taking a vitamin pills in isolation. Our bodies consist of approximately 63 per cent water, 22 per cent protein, 13 per cent fat and 2 per cent vitamins and minerals, and for optimum health we need to eat a balance of all the main food types – carbohydrates, proteins and fats.

Protein foods are made up of amino acids which improve brain function; they are also essential for muscle tone and growth, healthy skin and nails, for tissue repair and in the manufacture of hormones. They should make up 15–20 per cent of your daily diet. To help wake up your brain, always eat a healthy breakfast, such as eggs or soya milk or yoghurt with cereal, to reduce cravings and improve concentration. Vegetable-based proteins, such as lentils, kidney beans, soya bean curd, haricot beans, peas, corn, broccoli, runner beans and nuts (Brazil nuts, almonds, walnuts and pecans nuts are proteins), are preferable to animal-based proteins, as they are low in saturated (hard) fats and high in fibre. But again, as balance and variety are important, if you are not a vegetarian you can also enjoy fresh fish, eggs and chicken, and a little meat (preferably organic).

Unrefined, fibre-rich carbohydrates, such as brown rice, millet, rye, wholemeal or oat-based cereals, wholegrain breads, pasta and pulses, and whole foods, such as vegetables and fruits, contain natural sugars, which help to control mood swings. They also encourage production of the brain chemical serotonin which helps to calm the body and mind. These types of foods should make-up 60–70 per cent of your diet. Sugar is a carbohydrate, but after giving an initial energy burst, it can actually drain energy levels. Foods labelled 'low fat' often have a high sugar content, and sugar in excess converts to hard fat in the body if it is not burned up during exercise. So read labels carefully!

There is also a lot of misinformation regarding fats, and many people believe that low-fat or no-fat diets are healthier. In fact it's the type of fats we eat that is important. For optimum health a sufficient intake of certain fats (known as essential fatty acids, or EFAs) is necessary. These essential fats are needed by every cell in the body to function correctly. Sunflower, sesame and pumpkin seeds and linseeds and their unrefined oils, oily fish and avocados are all rich in EFAs.

Many processed foods, such as cakes, pies, sausages, margarines and hamburgers, contain hydrogenated or 'trans' fats, which should be avoided as much as possible as they cause the arteries to 'clog' thus reducing circulation. Avoid fried foods, and use extra virgin oil for stir fries and unrefined oils for salad dressings. Butter contains vitamin A and, although a saturated fat, it is preferable to mass-produced hydrogenated margarines. Fat, mainly in the form of essential fats, should make up 20–25 per cent of your daily diet.

Fruits and vegetables are packed with nutrients and fibre. Try to eat five types every day. Drink plenty of water, avoid excessive use of sodium-based salt and take some exercise every day. Learn to breathe more deeply – the mind and body work more efficiently when they have oxygenated blood circulating to the extremities. If we could introduce these ideas into our lives, many conditions, such as PMS and mood swings, could be prevented and in some cases cured. Nutritional scientists have known for almost 40 years that our state of mind is greatly influenced by the nutrients we absorb from our diet.

Fish and shellfish contain the amino acid tyrosine, used to make brain-stimulating chemicals that increase mental alertness.

Remember, your body is capable of healing itself when given the right tools for the job. Every 72 hours your gut lining is completely replaced, every month your skin is renewed, every two years you manufacture a new skeleton and a new liver. Our mind and body strive to maintain a healthy balance, but once a brain cell dies it's gone forever. Our aim in this book is to help you look after the few billion you have left and to help rebalance your mind and moods.

what are mind *and* mood foods *and* how do they work?

PRACTISE MIND CONTROL! *The brain is as dependent on nourishment as any other part of the body. The quality and type of food that we eat can affect the brain's chemical processes, and consequently influence the way we feel. By carefully selecting what you eat, you will be able to shift your mood, feel more alert, induce calmness, encourage sleep and reduce stress.*

Protein

Proteins are linked to motivation and clear thinking. Protein foods satisfy the appetite for a longer time than carbohydrates and, as a result, keep blood glucose well balanced when eaten in a meal that includes carbohydrates and fats. If you need to be wide awake and in top form, eat a balanced diet that includes protein foods at breakfast and/or lunch. Scrambled eggs, omelettes, soya milk, yoghurt, cheese, tuna, sardines, all kinds of beans, chicken and lean meat are all top-class protein providers.

Sometimes, protein foods eaten at night may encourage the brain to be over-active, which may keep you awake. This is because some protein foods contain amino acids that help to produce brain-stimulating chemicals.

Paradoxically, proteins also contain the essential amino acid tryptophan, which is associated with sleep. Milk is often given as a bedtime drink because of its tryptophan content and can, in fact, encourage sound sleep. Tryptophan is needed in the production of the brain chemical serotonin, which has a calming effect. However, although protein-based foods, such as poultry, cheese, meat and fish, are rich sources of tryptophan, it doesn't necessarily follow that tryptophan-rich foods will automatically induce calmness and sleep. That's because amino acids tend to 'compete' with each other for absorption, often leaving tryptophan last in line. In other words, it may not always be well absorbed. A meal containing carbohydrates can be better for increasing serotonin levels in the bloodstream.

Fish and shellfish contain an amino acid called tyrosine, used to make the brain-stimulating chemicals noradrenalin and dopamine, which increase mental energy and alertness. Oily fish contains omega-3 essential fatty acids, which are needed for the production of brain cells. Fish is also a worthwhile source of B group vitamins, needed for healthy brain and nerve function. Grilling, quick shallow frying, or baking are recommended methods for cooking fish.

Yoghurt is a great food for waking you up – best for breakfast or as a daytime snack.

Carbohydrates

Complex carbohydrates increase levels of serotonin, the brain chemical known for its calming properties. Feelings of serenity, security and tranquillity are all associated with adequate levels of serotonin. If you are like a coiled spring at the end of the day and need to wind down, it might help to eat brown rice, pasta, noodles, couscous and potato dishes with your evening meals. Try some of the more interesting pasta types such as corn, rice and legume. Complex carbohydrates might help ease anxiety, fretfulness, an overactive mind, irritability and sleeplessness. A small bowl of muesli or oat-based cereal, or a mashed banana (try it with a teaspoon of cold-pressed honey drizzled over), about an hour before bed, might help encourage a sound sleep.

Serotonin levels drop pre-menstrually, which may explain why women often feel more stressed, irritable, clumsy or depressed just before a period, and another reason why they suffer cravings for sweet and starchy foods.

Wholegrains such as oats, brown rice, rye, millet, barley and couscous are excellent suppliers of B group vitamins. Oats, usually associated with breakfast foods, are considered comfort food by some people, another reason why an oat-based cereal could make a soothing snack.

General guidelines

- If you want to stay awake and alert, eat proteins early in the day – at breakfast and at lunch.
- If you are feeling down, make sure your diet contains enough protein, but also increase your intake of fresh fruits, vegetables and pulses.
- If you are anxious or a worrier, try eating more complex carbohydrates.
- If you want to slow down and sleep, eat carbohydrates.
- If you're under a lot of stress, increase your intake of fresh fruits, vegetables and culinary herbs.
- Make vegetables and salads a major part of meals, not just a side dish.

Not-so-helpful foods

If you have food allergies or intolerances, or suffer from any gastrointestinal disease, the following foods may be upsetting.

Wheat and yeast

- Tend to be difficult to digest.

Cow's milk

- Cow's milk is difficult to digest for people suffering from lactose intolerance.
- Yoghurt is often tolerated by people with a lactose intolerance.
- Remember that many other foods also contain calcium.

Coffee, tea and cola

- Contain caffeine.

Food additives, especially colourings

- While food additives are extensively tested for safety and therefore present few problems, they are generally found in foods of poorer nutritional value.
- Read the labels on prepackaged foods.

Salt and sugar

- Keep salt to a minimum.
- Organic raw cane sugar, molasses, real maple syrup and cold-pressed honey are flavourful alternatives to white sugar but do not have significantly more nutritional value.

Regular mealtimes

Did you know that the brain has complete priority over the rest of the body when it comes to nourishment? That's why, when we haven't eaten and blood glucose levels have fallen, the first faculties to fail are concentration and memory. We're more likely to be irritable, anxious or suddenly very low. Eating balanced meals helps keep blood glucose on an even keel, sustaining concentration and co-ordination. We should include wholegrains in well-balanced meals and snacks so that energy-yielding nutrients are gradually released into the system, avoiding fast-release foods, such as high-fat and high-sugar fast foods.

Improve digestion and absorption

In order to break down foods that are difficult to digest, more blood has to be diverted to the digestive system. This means that the brain's blood supply is reduced, affecting brain function. One reason why people often doze after a heavy lunch is because the body is working hard on breaking down the meal, and the brain isn't functioning as well as it might.

Tips

- Eat balanced meals.
- Don't prepare huge portions.
- Don't eat on the run.
- Sit down to eat.
- Chew food really thoroughly.
- Leave a few minutes (or longer) between courses.
- Stay seated for five minutes or so after the last mouthful.
- Drink a small glass of water or other fluid with each meal.
- Remember to drink water throughout the day.
- If you're rushed and stressed, eat a light snack, such as fresh fruit, salad or soup, instead of a full meal. Eat a proper meal when you have time to enjoy it and are feeling calmer. Stress can seriously disturb digestion.

Vitamins and minerals

B group vitamins

B group vitamins are essential for healthy brain function. A lack of them is known to affect mental processing, perception, judgement, memory and reasoning. Deficiencies have also been linked to depression, nervousness, anxiety and low resistance to stress.

B_1

B_1 (thiamin) helps convert carbohydrates to energy and supports nerve function. A vitamin B_1 deficiency may cause poor concentration, difficulty in recalling information, weakness, low morale and mental confusion.

B_2

B_2 (riboflavin) is important for energy metabolism.

B_3

B_3 (niacin) is part of an enzyme that helps metabolise energy. Nervous tension, poor concentration, clouded judgement, bad memory, irritability, dizziness and mental confusion are common features of a lack of B_3. Along with B_6, magnesium and the amino acid tryptophan, B_3 is needed to produce serotonin.

B_5

B_5 (pantothenic acid) is used for energy metabolism and vital for the support of the adrenal glands. It is also needed for a healthy nervous system. Fatigue and insomnia are classic signs of deficiency.

B_6

B_6 (pyridoxine) is vital for protein metabolism and is known to improve mood. It is also important for immune function and the conversion of the amino acid tryptophan to the neurotransmitter serotonin. Low levels of B_6 can lead to an increase in homocysteine, an amino acid that is associated with heart disease. A B_6 deficiency may cause insomnia, irritability and fatigue.

B_{12}

B_{12} (cyanocobalamin) helps ensure a healthy nervous system. A severe deficiency of B_{12} can lead to permanent nerve and muscle damage.

folate

This B vitamin works closely with B_{12}, also with B_6 and vitamin C. A deficiency of folate may cause depression, mental confusion and fatigue. Research has shown that folic acid is vital during pregnancy to help prevent birth defects, such as spina bifida.

choline

Choline is not a true B vitamin, but acts like a B vitamin and plays a role in metabolism. Choline is needed for the production of a neurotransmitter (brain chemical) called acetylcholine and plays a role in memory function. Choline is found in many foods and is especially high in eggs and dairy products.

vitamin C

Vitamin C is well known as a major antioxidant, vital for a healthy immune system and for the production of hormones. The adrenal glands store vitamin C and, during emotional or physical stress, release the vitamin into the blood. Nearly all fruits and vegetables contain some vitamin C.

boron

Boron is a trace element needed by the body only in the tiniest amounts. It is essential for energy metabolism. A deficiency of boron has been linked to decreased mental alertness.

calcium and magnesium

Although calcium and magnesium are better known for bone and heart health, they are also vital for a healthy nervous system. Deficiencies of calcium or magnesium can have a profound effect upon the nervous system.

iron

Researchers are investigating the links between iron deficiency and depression, learning and memory.

selenium

The levels of selenium in food can vary depending on the selenium content of the soil it was grown in.

zinc

A severe zinc deficiency can impair the central nervous system and brain function.

essential fatty acids

Essential fatty acids (EFAs) are polyunsaturated fats that must be supplied in the diet because the body cannot make them itself. They are needed by every cell in the body and necessary for healthy brain tissue and an efficient nervous system. All kinds of vegetable oils, wheat germ, oily fish, meat, nuts and seeds are good sources of EFAs.

Fruit

Fruit is rich in fibre, antioxidants, boron, potassium, selenium, carotenoids and vitamin C.

apples

- Fibre
- Pectin
- Potassium
- Vitamin C

apricots

- Beta carotene
- Flavonoids
- Vitamin C

avocados

- B group vitamins
- Essential fatty acids
- Folate
- Iron
- Magnesium
- Vitamin C
- Vitamin E

bananas

- Folate
- Magnesium
- Pectin
- Potassium
- Vitamin C
- Vitamin B_2
- Vitamin B_6

blackberries

- Fibre
- Magnesium
- Vitamin C

blackcurrants

- Antioxidants
- B group vitamins
- Flavonoids
- Vitamin C

blueberries

- Antioxidants
- Vitamin C

carambolas (star fruit)

- Carotenoids
- Potassium
- Vitamin C

cherries

- Carotenoids
- Vitamin C

dried fruit

- B group vitamins
- Beta carotene
- Boron
- Fibre
- Iron
- Magnesium
- Potassium

figs

- B group vitamins
- Calcium
- Fibre
- Iron
- Magnesium

grapefruit

- Flavonoids
- Vitamin C

grapes

- Flavonoids
- Vitamin C

guavas

- Vitamin C

kiwifruit

- Calcium
- Fibre
- Magnesium
- Small amounts of iron and B group vitamins
- Vitamin C

kumquats

- Vitamin C

lemons

- Flavonoids
- Vitamin C

limes

- Vitamin C

mangoes

- Carotenoids
- Vitamin C

melons

- Beta carotene (particularly cantaloupe or orange-fleshed melons)
- Flavonoids
- Folate
- Vitamin B_6
- Vitamin C

nectarines

- Carotenoids
- Vitamin C

oranges

- Folate
- Vitamin B_1
- Vitamin C

papayas (pawpaws)

- Carotenoids
- Flavonoids
- Vitamin C

peaches

- Carotenoids
- Vitamin C

pineapples

- Vitamin B_1
- Vitamin C
- Natural digestive enzymes which help to break down other food

raspberries

- Antioxidants
- B group vitamins
- Fibre
- Iron
- Vitamin C

strawberries

- Antioxidants
- B group vitamins
- Carotenoids
- Vitamin C

watermelons

- Carotenoids

Vegetables

Vegetables provide vitamin C, fibre, potassium and carotenoids. Dark green leafy vegetables can be around six times richer in carotenoids, calcium, vitamin C and iron than paler varieties.

Yellow, orange and red vegetables, such as carrots, red and yellow peppers (capsicums), pumpkins and squashes, are abundant in carotenoids (which include beta carotene and lycopene), fibre, phenols (antioxidants) and vitamin C.

The brassicas include Brussels sprouts, all kinds of cabbage, Chinese broccoli, green and purple broccoli/calabrese, cauliflower and kale. Brassicas supply a few B vitamins, calcium, fibre, folate, iron, magnesium, selenium, silica, sulphoraphane, vitamin C and vitamin E.

Green vegetables are rich in antioxidants, B group vitamins, boron, calcium, iron, magnesium, selenium, vitamin C, vitamin E and zinc. Root vegetables are excellent sources of B group vitamins, calcium and selenium.

alfalfa sprouts

- Vitamin C

artichokes

- Beta carotene
- Folate
- Most minerals
- Diuretic
- Good for the digestion
- Contains cyanarin which is believed to protect the liver

asparagus

- Antioxidants
- Beta carotene
- Chromium
- Iron
- Vitamin C
- Vitamin E
- Selenium
- Diuretic

bamboo shoots

- Trace amounts of calcium, iron and vitamin C

beans, green

- Vitamin C

beansprouts

- Iron
- Vitamin B_1
- Vitamin C

beetroot

- Folate
- Potassium
- Vitamin C

broccoli

- Antioxidants
- Beta carotene
- Calcium
- Flavonoids
- Folate
- Magnesium
- Potassium
- Selenium
- Vitamin C

cabbage

- Selenium
- Vitamin C

carrots

- B group vitamins
- Beta carotene
- Calcium
- Carotenoids
- Fibre

cauliflower

- Vitamin C

celery

- Vitamin C

dandelion leaves

- Diuretic

garlic

- Anti-bacterial and anti-fungal
- Lowers cholesterol
- Selenium

kelp

- Zinc

mushrooms

- Selenium

onions

- Selenium
- Vitamin C

parsley

- Beta carotene
- Digestive aid
- Diuretic
- Folate
- Iron
- Potassium
- Vitamin C

peppers (capsicums)

- Beta carotene
- Vitamin C

potatoes

- Vitamin C
- Zinc

pumpkin

- Beta carotene
- Fibre

spinach

- Beta carotene
- Folate
- Magnesium

squashes

- Carotenoids

sweet potatoes

- Beta carotene
- Potassium
- Vitamin B_6
- Vitamin C

tomatoes

- Fibre
- Lycopene
- Selenium
- Vitamin C

turnips

- Turnip tops: beta carotene and iron
- Vitamin C

watercress

- Iron
- Vitamin C

yams

- Beta carotene
- Vitamin B_6
- Vitamin C

Fish

Fresh fish is a good source of protein, and nutrients, such as B group vitamins, calcium, magnesium, selenium, tryptophan, tyrosine and zinc. Oily fish, such as sardines, mackerel, salmon, pilchards, tuna and trout, are rich in Omega-3 fatty acids, vitamin A and vitamins B_2, B_3, B_5, B_6, B_{12}, folate, biotin and vitamin E.

salmon

- Calcium
- Omega-3 essential fatty acids
- Vitamin A
- Vitamins B_1, B_2, B_3, B_5, B_6, B_{12}, folate and biotin
- Vitamin E

sardines

- B group vitamins
- Calcium
- Essential fatty acids
- Vitamin A
- Vitamin E
- Zinc

seafood

- Chromium
- Magnesium
- Selenium
- Tyrosine
- Zinc

Meat

Choose lean cuts of meat if possible.

lamb

- B group vitamins
- Iron
- Protein

lamb's kidney

- B group vitamins
- Selenium

lamb's liver

- B group vitamins
- Chromium
- Iron
- Selenium
- Vitamin A

poultry

- B group vitamins
- Protein
- Selenium
- Tryptophan
- Zinc

stock (made with bones)

- Calcium

Cereals and grains

Cereals and pasta supply carbohydrates. Carbohydrates are the main source of energy for the body.

barley

- B group vitamins
- Folate
- Magnesium

buckwheat flour

- B vitamins
- Zinc

millet

- B group vitamins
- Zinc

oats

- Essential fatty acids
- Good soluble fibre
- Iron
- Vitamins B_1, B_2, B_3, B_5, B_6, biotin, folate
- Vitamin E
- Zinc

pasta

- B vitamins
- Iron

rice (brown)

- Fibre
- Folate
- Magnesium
- Potassium
- Selenium
- Vitamin B_1
- Vitamin B_3
- Vitamin E
- Zinc

rye

- B group vitamins
- Zinc

wholegrains

- B group vitamins
- Chromium
- Iron
- Magnesium
- Selenium
- Vitamin E

Beans and pulses

Beans and pulses are a good source of protein, B group vitamins, iron and magnesium.

chickpeas

- B group vitamins
- Calcium
- Iron
- Vitamin A
- Vitamin C
- Zinc

lentils

- B group vitamins
- Iron
- Zinc

peas

- B group vitamins
- Carotene
- Iron
- Vitamin C
- Zinc

red kidney beans

- B group vitamins
- Zinc

soya beans

- B group vitamins
- Calcium
- Tofu (bean curd) – an excellent protein source for vegetarians: rich in calcium, magnesium, folate, iron.
- Zinc

Dairy products

Eggs, cheese and yoghurt supply the protein needed by the body for growth and repair.

butter

- Vitamin A

cheese

- Calcium
- Tryptophan
- Vitamin A
- Vitamin B_2
- Zinc

eggs

- B group vitamins
- Chromium
- Iron
- Selenium
- Vitamin A
- Vitamin D
- Vitamin E
- Zinc

yoghurt

- Calcium
- Yoghurt with live and active cultures may be beneficial to digestion and a valuable source of friendly flora.
- Magnesium
- Potassium
- Sheep's and goat's milk yoghurt provides easily digestible protein.
- Tryptophan
- Vitamin A
- Vitamins B_1 and B_2
- Zinc

Nuts

Nuts are a good source of B group vitamins, calcium, fibre, iron, magnesium, essential fatty acids, potassium, selenium and zinc.

almonds

- B group vitamins
- Calcium
- Fibre
- Iron
- Magnesium
- Monounsaturated and polyunsaturated fatty acids
- Omega-6 essential fatty acids
- Potassium
- Selenium
- Zinc

Brazil nuts

- B group vitamins
- Calcium
- Fibre
- Iron
- Magnesium
- Monounsaturated and polyunsaturated fatty acids
- Omega-6 essential fatty acids
- Potassium
- Selenium
- Zinc

cashew nuts

- B group vitamins
- Calcium
- Essential fatty acids
- Fibre
- Iron
- Magnesium
- Potassium
- Selenium
- Zinc

hazelnuts

- B group vitamins
- Boron
- Fibre
- Iron
- Magnesium
- Monounsaturated and polyunsaturated fatty acids
- Omega-6 essential fatty acids
- Potassium
- Selenium
- Zinc

macadamia nuts

- B group vitamins
- Boron
- Calcium
- Fibre
- Iron
- Magnesium
- Monounsaturated and polyunsaturated fatty acids
- Omega-6 essential fatty acids
- Potassium
- Selenium
- Zinc

walnuts

- B group vitamins
- Calcium
- Fibre
- Iron
- Magnesium
- Omega-3 essential fatty acids
- Potassium
- Selenium
- Zinc

Seeds

Edible seeds include pumpkin, sesame, sunflower, poppy, celery, dill and fennel seeds and flaxseeds and linseeds. They contain B group vitamins, calcium, essential fatty acids, iron, magnesium, potassium, vitamin E and zinc.

linseeds

- Iron
- Magnesium
- Omega-3 essential fatty acids
- Potassium
- Zinc

pumpkin seeds

- Iron
- Magnesium
- Omega-3 essential fatty acids
- Omega-6 essential fatty acids
- Potassium
- Zinc

sesame seeds

- Calcium
- Essential fatty acids
- Iron
- Magnesium
- Potassium
- Zinc

sunflower seeds

- Calcium
- Iron
- Magnesium
- Omega-6 essential fatty acids
- Potassium
- Vitamin E
- Zinc

Oils

Oils contain monounsaturated and polyunsaturated fatty acids.

almond oil

- Omega-6 essential fatty acids

cold-pressed oils

- Cold-pressed oils include sunflower, sesame, walnut, safflower, soya bean and linseed oils and extra-virgin olive oil.
- Essential fatty acids
- Vitamin E

fish oils

- Essential fatty acids
- Vitamin A
- Vitamin D

Sugars

Sugars are carbohydrates.

blackstrap molasses

- Iron

honey

- Same nutritional profile as sugar
- Anti-bacterial
- Helps wounds to heal

notes *on* ingredients

Whenever possible, use fresh vegetables, fruit and juices. Organically grown produce is preferable as it is free from chemical fertilisers and pesticides. Cooking vegetables by steaming or microwaving is the best way to retain their nutrients.

Organic dairy products – milk, butter, cheese and yoghurt – are available in health food shops and major supermarkets. For cooking, thick, creamy Greek-style yoghurt has the best consistency. People who are allergic to or intolerant of cow's milk can use goat's milk, and sheep's or goat's milk yoghurt. Although no significant nutritional difference between organic and intensively farmed produce has yet been proved, you may prefer to use free-range lamb, poultry and eggs.

Although only an extremely small percentage of eggs contain salmonella bacteria – which, if the eggs are improperly handled, can multiply and cause salmonellosis – it is worth noting that mayonnaise and dishes that call for uncooked eggs can possibly cause illness. To reduce this risk greatly, buy only very fresh eggs in unbroken shells, refrigerate them immediately, and use them as quickly as possible. Wash your hands and all work surfaces and utensils thoroughly before working with eggs. It is best to avoid uncooked eggs altogether if you will be serving children, elderly people, or those with a compromised immune system, or if you live in an area that has experienced outbreaks of salmonellosis.

When a recipe includes olive oil, the best kind to use is extra virgin olive oil. Because it is produced by pressure, rather than by chemical processing, it is thought that more of the antioxidants are preserved to give better nutritional value and flavour. Oils, such as sunflower, sesame, hazelnut and walnut, should be unrefined and cold-pressed. Most mass-produced cooking oils are processed using heat and solvents. Cold-pressed and unrefined oils are more expensive, but are claimed to retain more of the natural goodness of the oils, in particular the essential fatty acids, or EFAs, and vitamin E.

The use of white sugar should be kept to a minimum. Organic brown sugar, molasses, real maple syrup and cold-pressed honey are alternatives that should be used in moderation.

Wholegrains, such as brown rice, oats, rye, millet, barley and couscous, are excellent sources of fibre and B group vitamins. Breads served with a meal should be of the wholegrain variety. For people with gluten sensitivity, gluten-free flours and pasta, made from potato, rice, buckwheat or legumes, are available.

Soy sauce contains some useful minerals, but these include high levels of sodium. Being careful of your salt intake is important if you have high blood pressure. None of the recipes in this book include more than a tablespoon of soy sauce, but some people may prefer to use the reduced-salt version.

notes *on the* recipes

Both metric and imperial measurements are given in the recipes. Use one set of measurements only throughout a recipe, because metric and imperial measurements are not interchangeable. The preparation and cooking times are approximate.

All spoon measurements refer to British Standard measuring spoons. All spoonfuls are level, unless otherwise stated.

1 teaspoon (tsp) = 5ml
1 tablespoon (tbsp) = 15ml (3 teaspoons)

As the Australian tablespoon is 20ml (4 teaspoons), Australian readers should use 3 teaspoons whenever a tablespoon is specified (New Zealand uses British spoons).

Ovens and grills should be preheated to the temperature specified in the recipe. The cooking times for all the recipes in this book are based on the oven or grill being preheated. If using a fan oven, follow the manufacturer's instructions for adjusting the time and temperature.

Frozen dishes may be defrosted in the microwave, or left for several hours or overnight in the refrigerator. *Do not thaw at room temperature unless instructed.*

Fresh herbs are used in many of the recipes. Fresh herbs give a better flavour, but if dried herbs are used instead of fresh, one tablespoon of finely chopped fresh herbs is equivalent to about one teaspoon of dried herbs. This does not apply to recipes where dried herbs only are listed, such as dried *herbes de provence:* a mixture of rosemary, thyme, sage, parsley and bay leaves.

basic recipes

home-made chicken stock

ingredients

- 1 meaty free-range chicken carcass
- 1 onion or 2 leeks, sliced
- 2 carrots, sliced
- 2 celery sticks, chopped
- 1 bay leaf or 1 fresh bouquet garni
- sea salt
- freshly ground black pepper

makes approx
700ml (1¼ pints)

method

1 Break or chop the chicken carcass into pieces and place in a large saucepan.
2 Add the prepared vegetables and bay leaf or bouquet garni with 1.7 litres (3 pints) cold water.
3 Bring to the boil, reduce the heat, then partially cover the pan and simmer gently for about 2 hours. Skim off and discard any scum and fat.
4 Strain the stock through a sieve, then set aside to cool. When cold, remove and discard all the fat.
5 When required for use, season to taste.

If not required immediately, this stock can be kept in the refrigerator in a covered container for up to 3 days, or frozen for up to 3 months.

home-made vegetable stock

ingredients

- 2 onions, sliced
- 1 large carrot, sliced
- 1 leek, sliced
- 4 sticks celery, chopped
- 1 small turnip or 115g (4oz) swede, diced
- 1 parsnip, sliced
- 1 fresh bouquet garni or 1 bay leaf
- sea salt
- freshly ground black pepper

makes approx
1.3 litres (2¼ pints)

method

1 Put the prepared vegetables and bouquet garni or bay leaf in a large saucepan. Add 1.7 litres (3 pints) cold water.
2 Bring to the boil, reduce the heat, then partially cover the pan and simmer gently for 1–1½ hours. Skim off and discard any scum that rises to the surface.
3 Strain the stock through a sieve.
4 Season to taste.

If not required immediately, this stock can be kept in the refrigerator in a covered container for up to 3 days, or frozen for up to 3 months.

mayonnaise

ingredients

- 2 egg yolks
- 1tsp Dijon mustard
- 1tbsp lemon or lime juice
- ½tsp sugar
- ½tsp sea salt
- freshly ground black pepper
- 150ml (¼ pint) olive oil

makes approx
200ml (7fl oz)

To reduce the risk of salmonella when using uncooked eggs, buy only very fresh eggs in unbroken shells, refrigerate them immediately, and use them as quickly as possible. Wash your hands and all work surfaces and utensils thoroughly before working with eggs. It is best to avoid uncooked eggs altogether if you will be serving children, elderly people, or anyone with a compromised immune system.

method

1 Put the egg yolks, mustard, lemon or lime juice, sugar, salt, black pepper and 1tbsp oil into a small blender or food processor. Blend for 30 seconds.

2 With the blades turning, gradually add the remaining oil, pouring it through the funnel in a slow, continuous stream, until the mayonnaise is thick and smooth.

3 Adjust the seasoning, then use immediately or cover and refrigerate for up to 3 days.

french dressing

ingredients

- 6tbsp olive oil
- 2tbsp white wine or cider vinegar, or lemon juice
- 1–2tsp Dijon mustard
- pinch of sugar
- 1 small clove garlic, crushed
- 1–2tbsp chopped fresh mixed herbs
- sea salt
- freshly ground black pepper

makes approx
150ml (¼ pint)

method

1 Put all the ingredients in a small bowl and whisk together until thoroughly mixed. Alternatively, put all the ingredients in a clean, screw-top jar, seal and shake well until thoroughly mixed.

2 Adjust the seasoning and serve immediately or keep in a screw-top jar in the refrigerator for up to 1 week. Shake thoroughly before serving.

In this section, you will find a large variety of foods that will help to feed your brain to encourage a sharper memory, and to improve alertness, clear thinking and concentration. For optimum functioning, the brain requires plenty of B group vitamins, and vitamin B_3 (niacin), B_5 (pantothenic acid) B_6 and B_{12}, which are found in liver, eggs and fish, are especially important for clear thinking. Wholegrains and cereals, such as barley and porridge, as well as split peas, brown rice, apricots, mushrooms and clams, are all rich in B vitamins. Essential fatty acids (EFAs), found in oily fish, such as sardines and mackerel, and in nuts and seeds, especially walnuts, Brazil nuts, sunflower seeds, pumpkin seeds and vegetable oils, are vital for the brain development of a growing foetus.

FOODS

Lack of EFAs in some children and adults can affect alertness, memory and concentration. Lecithin, a substance found in soya beans, other pulses, grains and egg yolks, is also being studied for its role in brain function. The minerals zinc, boron, calcium, magnesium and iron are all important brain nutrients – they are found in seafood, tofu, almonds, sesame seeds, raw wheat germ, dairy produce and blackstrap molasses. Vitamin C, found in citrus fruit, berries, green vegetables, red peppers and watercress, and to some extent in all fruits and vegetables, aids the absorption of minerals such as iron, which helps to energise the mind. You will find all these foods and more in our recipes – *bon appetit!*

brain *foods*

THE BRAIN TAKES *priority over the rest of the body when it comes to nourishment. That is why, when you haven't eaten and your blood glucose level drops, you are more likely to feel irritable, anxious or suddenly down in the dumps.*

The first faculties to fail are concentration, information storage, memory and recall. Eating balanced meals and snacks helps to keep blood glucose on an even keel. Choose wholegrains and other complex carbohydrates that release their natural sugars slowly into the system.

mixed bean *and* vegetable soup

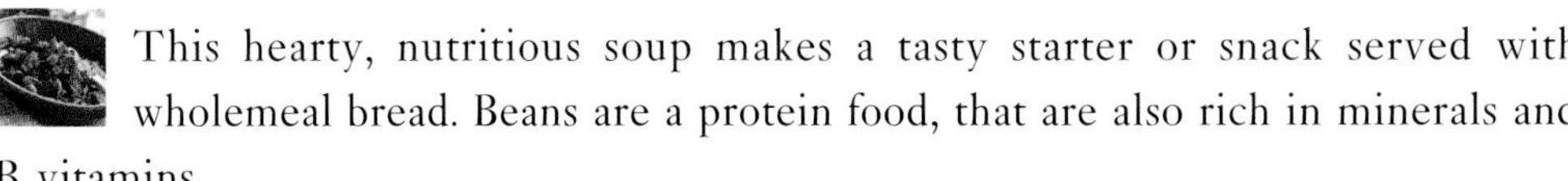

This hearty, nutritious soup makes a tasty starter or snack served with wholemeal bread. Beans are a protein food, that are also rich in minerals and B vitamins.

ingredients

- 2 leeks, washed and sliced
- 3 sticks celery, finely chopped
- 450g (1lb) mixed carrots, turnips and swede, diced
- 1 bulb fennel, diced
- 850ml (1½ pints) vegetable stock (see recipe on page 20)
- salt
- freshly ground black pepper
- 400g (14oz) can red kidney beans, rinsed and drained
- 400g (14oz) can chickpeas, rinsed and drained
- fresh coriander

serves *six*
preparation time *10 minutes*
cooking time *30 minutes*

method

1 Put the leeks, celery, carrots, turnips, swede and fennel in a large saucepan with the stock and seasoning, and stir.
2 Cover, bring to the boil, then reduce the heat and simmer for 20 minutes, stirring occasionally.
3 Stir in the kidney beans and chickpeas. Cover and simmer for a further 5–10 minutes until the vegetables and beans are cooked and tender, stirring occasionally.
4 Stir in 1–2tbsp chopped coriander, then ladle into warmed soup bowls to serve.
5 Garnish with coriander sprigs. Serve with wholemeal bread or rolls.

variations

- *Use canned flageolet or black-eye beans instead of red kidney beans.*
- *Use chopped fresh mixed herbs or parsley instead of coriander.*
- *Use 1 large onion instead of leeks.*
- *Use 225g (8oz) parsnips instead of the fennel.*

freezing instructions

Allow to cool completely, then transfer to a rigid, freezeproof container. Cover, seal and label. Freeze for up to 3 months. Defrost, and reheat gently in a saucepan until piping hot.

crab *and* sweetcorn chowder

This delicious fish chowder makes an ideal starter or snack for chilly days. Crab provides zinc, which is needed by the brain for mental alertness, memory and concentration.

ingredients

- 1tbsp olive oil
- 1 onion, chopped
- 1 clove garlic, crushed
- 4 sticks celery, chopped
- 1 small green pepper (capsicum), seeded and diced
- 350g (12oz) potatoes, diced
- 175g (6oz) button mushrooms, sliced
- 450ml (16fl oz) vegetable stock (see recipe on page 20)
- 300ml (½ pint) milk
- 225g (8oz) canned sweetcorn kernels (drained weight)
- 225g (8oz) white crabmeat, flaked
- salt
- freshly ground black pepper
- 2tbsp chopped fresh parsley
- fresh parsley sprigs, to garnish

serves ***six***
preparation time ***15 minutes***
cooking time ***25–30 minutes***

method

1 Heat the oil in a large saucepan. Add the onion, garlic, celery and green pepper and cook for 5 minutes, stirring occasionally.
2 Stir in the potatoes, mushrooms and stock. Cover, bring to the boil, then reduce the heat and simmer for 15–20 minutes, until the vegetables are just cooked and tender, stirring occasionally.
3 Add the milk, sweetcorn, crabmeat and seasoning. Bring gently back to the boil, then simmer for 5 minutes, stirring.
4 Add the chopped parsley, then ladle into soup bowls.
5 Garnish with the parsley sprigs and serve with wholemeal bread rolls.

variations

- *Use canned crabmeat, drained and flaked, if fresh crabmeat is not available.*
- *Use canned salmon or tuna, drained and flaked, instead of crab.*
- *Use frozen petit pois (baby peas) instead of canned sweetcorn.*

asparagus *with* hazelnuts

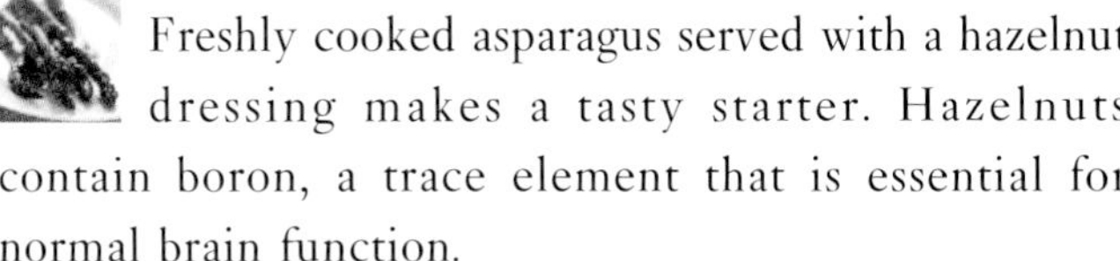

Freshly cooked asparagus served with a hazelnut dressing makes a tasty starter. Hazelnuts contain boron, a trace element that is essential for normal brain function.

ingredients

- 450g (1lb) asparagus, trimmed
- 25–55g (1–2oz) toasted hazelnuts, roughly chopped
- fresh coriander sprigs, to garnish

for the dressing

- 2tbsp hazelnut oil
- 1tbsp olive oil
- 1tbsp lemon juice
- 1tbsp honey
- 1tsp Dijon mustard
- 2 spring onions, finely chopped
- 1 clove garlic, crushed
- 1tbsp chopped fresh coriander
- sea salt
- freshly ground black pepper

serves ***four***
preparation time ***10 minutes***
cooking time ***8–12 minutes***

method

1 Tie the asparagus in small bundles and cook upright in a deep saucepan of lightly salted, boiling water for 8–12 minutes, until tender. Ensure that the tips are above the water so that they are steamed rather than boiled.
2 To make the dressing, put the oils, lemon juice, honey, mustard, spring onions, garlic, chopped coriander and seasoning in a bowl and whisk together.
3 Drain the asparagus, untie the bundles and divide the stalks between four serving plates.
4 Drizzle the dressing over the asparagus, scatter some hazelnuts over each portion and garnish with the coriander sprigs.
5 Serve immediately with crusty wholemeal bread.

variations

- *Use walnut oil and walnuts instead of hazelnut oil and hazelnuts.*
- *Use chopped fresh parsley instead of coriander.*

fish *with* broccoli sauce

White fish served with a delicious fresh broccoli sauce makes a nutritious and appetising meal. Broccoli is a good source of vitamin C, an important nutrient that aids the absorption of iron.

ingredients

- 6 firm white fish steaks, such as haddock or gemfish, each weighing about 175g (6oz)
- sea salt
- freshly ground black pepper
- juice of 2 lemons
- fresh herb sprigs, to garnish

for the sauce

- 225g (8oz) broccoli florets
- 1 small onion, chopped
- 15g (½oz) butter
- 15g (½oz) plain wholemeal flour
- 150ml (¼ pint) milk
- 150ml (¼ pint) vegetable stock, cooled (see recipe on page 20)
- 55g (2oz) Cheddar cheese, finely grated

serves *six*
preparation time *10 minutes*
cooking time *20–30 minutes*

method

1 Preheat the oven to 180°C/350°F/gas mark 4.
2 Place each fish steak on a piece of baking paper. Season, then sprinkle over lemon juice. Fold the paper to make parcels.
3 Place on a baking tray and bake for 20–30 minutes, until the fish is just cooked.
4 Cook the broccoli and onion in boiling water for about 7 minutes, until tender. Drain, then blend in a food processor with 3tbsp of the cooking liquid.
5 Put the butter, flour, milk and stock in a saucepan and heat gently, whisking continuously, until the sauce comes to the boil and thickens. Simmer gently for 3 minutes, then stir in the broccoli purée and reheat gently.
6 Remove from the heat, stir in the cheese, then season to taste. Pour over the fish to serve.
7 Garnish with the herb sprigs and serve with cooked vegetables.

variations

- *Use fresh spinach instead of broccoli.*

cajun-spiced seafood stir-fry

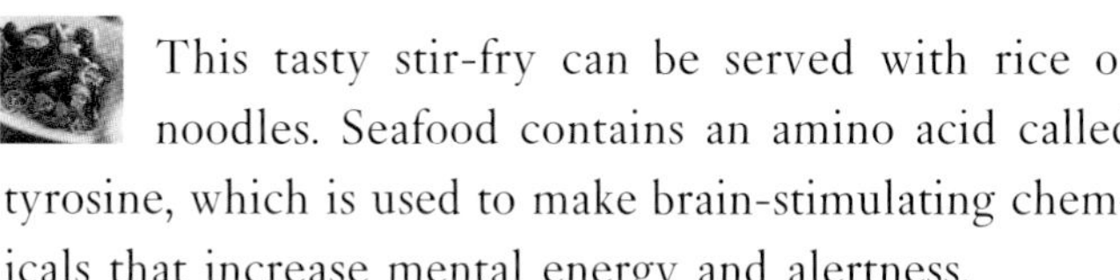

This tasty stir-fry can be served with rice or noodles. Seafood contains an amino acid called tyrosine, which is used to make brain-stimulating chemicals that increase mental energy and alertness.

ingredients

- 20ml (4tsp) cajun seasoning
- 30ml (2tbsp) dry sherry
- 15ml (1tbsp) light soy sauce
- 15ml (1tbsp) tomato purée (paste)
- freshly ground black pepper
- 1tbsp olive oil
- 2 cloves garlic, crushed
- 2 carrots, cut into matchstick (julienne) strips
- 1 yellow pepper (capsicum), seeded and sliced
- 350g (12oz) mixed raw, shelled, prepared seafood, such as mussels, prawns, scallops and squid
- 2 courgettes (zucchini), cut into matchstick (julienne) strips
- 6–8 spring onions, chopped

serves *four*
preparation time *15 minutes*
cooking time *8–10 minutes*

method

1 Mix the cajun seasoning, sherry, soy sauce, tomato purée and black pepper together in a small bowl and set aside.
2 Heat the oil in a non-stick wok or large frying pan. Add the garlic, carrots and pepper and stir-fry over a high heat for 2 minutes.
3 Add the mixed seafood, courgettes and spring onions, and stir-fry for a further 4–6 minutes.
4 Add the cajun seasoning mixture and stir-fry until the seafood and vegetables are cooked and tender and everything is piping hot.
5 Serve with brown rice, egg noodles or rice noodles.

variations

- *Use parsnips instead of carrots.*
- *Use chinese 5-spice seasoning instead of cajun seasoning.*
- *Use sesame oil instead of olive oil.*

poached salmon *with* celery sauce

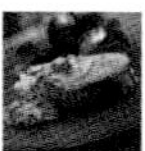

Fresh salmon steaks served with a tasty celery sauce make a tempting dish. Salmon is a good source of omega-3 fatty acids, important for brain function.

ingredients

- 6 salmon steaks, each weighing about 175g (6oz)
- vegetable stock (see recipe on page 20), for poaching
- fresh parsley sprigs, to garnish

for the sauce

- 25g (1oz) butter
- 3 shallots (French shallots), finely chopped
- 4 sticks celery, finely chopped
- 2tbsp cornflour
- 350ml (12fl oz) milk
- 2tbsp chopped fresh parsley
- sea salt
- freshly ground black pepper

serves *six*
preparation time *10 minutes*
cooking time *15–20 minutes*

method

1 Place the salmon steaks in a large, deep frying pan and pour over enough stock to cover the fish completely. Cover, bring to the boil, then reduce the heat and simmer gently for about 10 minutes, until the salmon is cooked and the flesh just flakes when tested with a fork.

2 Meanwhile, melt the butter in a saucepan. Add the shallots and celery, cover and cook for 15–20 minutes, until the vegetables are tender, stirring occasionally.

3 Blend the cornflour with a little of the milk, then stir in the remaining milk. Bring to the boil, stirring continuously, until the sauce comes to the boil and thickens. Simmer gently for 2 minutes, stirring continuously.

4 Stir in the hot cooked vegetables and chopped parsley. Season to taste.

5 Using a slotted spoon or fish slice, carefully remove the salmon steaks from the stock and place on warmed serving plates. Discard the stock.

6 Spoon some celery sauce over the fish, or alongside, and garnish with the parsley sprigs.

7 Serve with cooked fresh vegetables, such as new potatoes, carrots and broccoli.

variations

- *Use tuna steaks instead of salmon.*
- *Use chopped fresh chives or tarragon instead of parsley.*
- *Use 1 onion instead of shallots.*

honey *and* mustard chicken drumsticks

Chicken drumsticks coated with honey and mustard are a popular choice with many families. Protein foods such as chicken contain amino acids that help produce brain-stimulating chemicals.

ingredients

- 3tbsp honey
- 2tbsp wholegrain mustard
- 1tbsp olive oil
- 1tbsp fresh lemon juice
- 1 clove garlic, crushed
- sea salt
- freshly ground black pepper
- 8 skinless chicken drumsticks
- fresh herb sprigs, to garnish

serves ***four***
(two drumsticks each)
preparation time *10 minutes*
cooking time *20–25 minutes*

method

1 Preheat the grill to high.
2 Put the honey, mustard, olive oil, lemon juice, garlic and seasoning in a small bowl and whisk thoroughly.
3 Cut three slashes in each chicken drumstick, place them on a grill rack and brush each one all over with some of the honey mixture.
4 Grill for 20–25 minutes, until the chicken is cooked through and tender, turning frequently and basting with the honey mixture.
5 Serve hot or cold, garnished with the herb sprigs.
6 Serve with oven-baked potatoes and home-made crunchy coleslaw.

variations

- *Use lime or orange juice instead of lemon juice.*
- *Use lean lamb cutlets or chops instead of chicken drumsticks.*

grilled lamb kebabs *with* mint salsa

Kebabs are always popular, especially in the summertime, when they can be cooked on a barbecue and enjoyed alfresco. Protein foods such as lamb contain amino acids that help produce brain-stimulating chemicals.

ingredients

for the kebabs

- 350g (12oz) lean lamb, cut into 2.5cm (1in) cubes
- 1tbsp olive oil
- 2tbsp fresh lemon juice
- 1tbsp chopped fresh mint
- sea salt and ground black pepper
- 1 small red pepper (capsicum), seeded and cut into 8 pieces
- 1 small yellow pepper (capsicum), seeded and cut into 8 pieces
- 16 button mushrooms
- 8 baby (pickling) onions, halved
- fresh herb sprigs, to garnish

for the salsa

- 1tbsp olive oil
- 2tbsp chopped fresh mint
- 450g (1lb) tomatoes, skinned, seeded and finely chopped
- 2 shallots (French shallots), finely chopped
- 1 clove garlic, crushed
- 1tsp balsamic vinegar

serves *four*
preparation time *15 minutes, plus 1 hour for marination*
cooking time *10–15 minutes*

method

1 Place the lamb in a shallow, non-metallic dish. In a small bowl, whisk together the olive oil, lemon juice, mint and seasoning. Pour over the lamb and mix well. Cover and refrigerate for 1 hour.

2 To make the salsa, mix the olive oil, mint, tomatoes, shallots, garlic and vinegar in a bowl. Season, cover and set aside for 1 hour to allow the flavours to blend.

3 Thread the lamb, peppers, mushrooms and baby onions onto skewers. Reserve the marinade.

4 Preheat the grill to medium. Place the lamb kebabs on a rack in a grill pan and grill for 10–15 minutes, until the lamb is cooked, turning occasionally. Brush the kebabs with the reserved marinade, to prevent drying out.

5 Serve the kebabs on a bed of herbed brown rice, with the mint salsa alongside.

6 Garnish with the herb sprigs and serve with a mixed dark-green leaf salad.

variations

- *Use skinless chicken or turkey breast instead of lamb.*
- *Use fresh basil instead of mint.*
- *Use shallots instead of baby onions.*

potato, onion *and* herb bake

This mouthwatering potato bake makes an ideal light meal. The potato skin adds extra flavour and texture. Potatoes and parsley provide vitamin C, which helps with the absorption of iron, an important brain nutrient.

ingredients

- 700g (1lb 9oz) potatoes, scrubbed and thinly sliced
- 2 onions, thinly sliced
- 2tbsp chopped fresh parsley
- 2tbsp chopped fresh chives
- sea salt
- freshly ground black pepper
- 6tbsp milk
- 25g (1oz) butter
- fresh parsley sprigs, to garnish

serves *four*
preparation time *20 minutes*
cooking time *about 1 hour 45 minutes*

method

1 Preheat the oven to 180°C/350°F/gas mark 4.

2 Grease an ovenproof casserole dish. Add a thin layer of potatoes over the base, top with a layer of onions, sprinkle over some parsley and chives, then season with salt and pepper. Continue these layers until all the ingredients are used up, finishing with a layer of potato.

3 Pour the milk over the potatoes and dot the top with butter.

4 Cover with foil and bake for 1 hour, then remove the foil and bake uncovered for a further 30–45 minutes, until the vegetables are cooked and tender and the top is lightly browned.

5 Garnish with the parsley sprigs and serve with mixed grilled vegetables, such as peppers (capsicums), courgettes (zucchini) and aubergines (eggplants).

variations

- *Use sweet potatoes or a mixture of standard and sweet potatoes.*
- *Use 2 red onions instead of standard onions.*

warm rice *and* vegetable salad

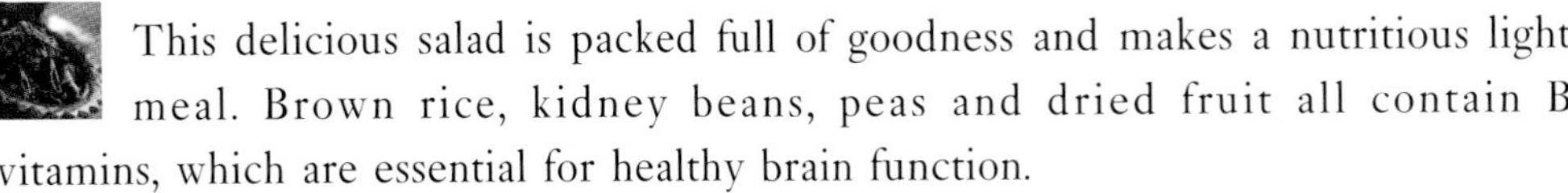

This delicious salad is packed full of goodness and makes a nutritious light meal. Brown rice, kidney beans, peas and dried fruit all contain B vitamins, which are essential for healthy brain function.

ingredients

- 225g (8oz) long grain brown rice
- 115g (4oz) frozen peas
- 4tbsp olive oil
- 2 shallots (French shallots), finely chopped
- 1 fresh red chilli, seeded and finely chopped
- 6tbsp passata (sieved tomatoes)
- 2tbsp red wine vinegar
- 1tsp Dijon mustard
- sea salt
- freshly ground black pepper
- 55g (2oz) watercress, chopped
- 1 red pepper (capsicum), seeded and diced
- 6–8 spring onions, chopped
- 85g (3oz) sultanas
- 85g (3oz) ready-to-eat dried apricots, chopped
- 400g (14oz) can red kidney beans, rinsed and drained
- fresh herb sprigs, to garnish

serves *six*
preparation time *15 minutes*
cooking time *35 minutes*

method

1 Boil the rice until cooked and tender.

2 Meanwhile, cook the peas in boiling water for about 3 minutes, until cooked and tender. Drain thoroughly and set aside.

3 Heat 1tbsp oil in a saucepan. Add the shallots and chilli and cook for 5 minutes.

4 Put the cooked shallots and chilli in a blender or food processor with the remaining oil, passata, vinegar, mustard and seasoning and blend until smooth. Set aside.

5 Put the peas, watercress, red pepper, spring onions, dried fruit and kidney beans in a large bowl and stir.

6 Rinse and drain the cooked rice, and stir into the vegetables.

7 Pour over the chilli dressing and toss thoroughly.

8 Garnish with the herb sprigs and serve with wholemeal bread.

variations

- *The salad may be served cold.*
- *Use tomato juice instead of passata.*
- *Use rocket instead of watercress.*

banana *and* pecan muffins

These muffins are quick and easy to make for afternoon tea or breakfast. Nuts provide protein, iron and other nutrients vital for healthy brain function.

ingredients

- 140g (5oz) plain wholemeal flour
- 55g (2oz) fine oatmeal
- 1tbsp baking powder
- pinch of salt
- 55g (2oz) pecan nuts, chopped
- 55g (2oz) butter, melted
- 55g (2oz) light brown sugar
- 1 medium egg, beaten
- 200ml (7fl oz) milk
- 1 large banana, peeled and mashed with a little lemon juice

makes *nine*
preparation time *20 minutes*
cooking time *20 minutes*

method

1 Preheat the oven to 200°C/400°F/gas mark 6.
2 Line 9 muffin tins with paper cases.
3 Put the flour, oatmeal, baking powder, salt and pecan nuts in a bowl and stir.
4 Mix the melted butter, sugar, egg and milk in a separate bowl, then pour over the flour mixture.
5 Gently fold the ingredients together, then fold in the banana.
6 Spoon the mixture into the paper cases, filling each case two-thirds full. Bake for about 20 minutes, or until risen and golden brown.
7 Transfer to a wire rack to cool. Serve the muffins warm or cold, plain or split and spread with a little butter or honey.

variations

- *Use walnuts instead of pecans.*
- *Use 115g (4oz) dried fruit such as sultanas, raisins or chopped ready-to-eat dried apricots or pears instead of the banana.*
- *Use 115g (4oz) fresh blackberries, blueberries or chopped strawberries instead of the banana.*

salad *of* golden fruits

Fresh golden fruits served in a mixture of fruit juices make a delicious dessert. Orange-fleshed melons are a good source of folate and vitamin C.

ingredients

- 200ml (7fl oz) unsweetened apple juice
- 200ml (7fl oz) unsweetened orange juice
- 2tbsp apricot brandy
- 1 small orange-fleshed melon
- 1 small pineapple
- 1 peach or nectarine
- 6 apricots
- 1 papaya (pawpaw)
- fresh mint sprigs or toasted, flaked almonds, to decorate

serves *six*
preparation time *20 minutes, plus 1–2 hours standing time*

method

1 Put the apple juice, orange juice and apricot brandy in a serving bowl and stir.
2 Peel and seed the melon and dice the flesh. Peel and core the pineapple and dice the flesh. Peel and stone the peach or nectarine and chop the flesh. Add the chopped fruit to the juice mixture.
3 Halve, stone and slice the apricots. Peel and seed the papaya and slice or chop the flesh. Add to the serving bowl and stir gently.
4 Cover and leave to stand at room temperature for 1–2 hours before serving, to allow the flavours to blend.
5 Decorate with the mint sprigs or toasted, flaked almonds and serve with plain yoghurt.

variations

- *Use other mixed fresh fruits.*
- *Use pineapple or white grape juice instead of apple juice.*

blackberry *and* apple streusel

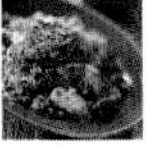

Fresh apples and blackberries with a crunchy oat topping make a rich, sweet treat for all the family. Fruit is a good source of vitamin C. Oats contain B vitamins, which are important brain nutrients.

ingredients

- 115g (4oz) plain wholemeal flour
- 115g (4oz) light brown sugar
- 115g (4oz) butter, chopped
- 55g (2oz) rolled oats
- 1tsp ground cinnamon
- 350g (12oz) ripe blackberries
- 450g (1lb) eating apples (peeled and cored weight), thinly sliced
- finely grated rind of 1 lemon
- 2tbsp unsweetened red grape juice
- 2tbsp honey

serves *four to six*
preparation time *15 minutes*
cooking time *30 minutes*

method

1 Preheat the oven to 190°C/375°F/gas mark 5.
2 Put the flour and sugar in a bowl and lightly rub in the chopped butter until the mixture resembles coarse crumbs. Stir in the oats and ground cinnamon.
3 Put the blackberries, apples and lemon rind in an ovenproof dish and stir.
4 Mix together the grape juice and honey and pour over the fruit.
5 Spoon the oat streusel mixture evenly over the fruit.
6 Bake for about 30 minutes, or until the fruit is cooked and the streusel topping is golden brown and crunchy.
7 Serve hot or cold with home-made custard or plain yoghurt.

variations

- *Use raspberries or blueberries instead of blackberries.*
- *Use medium oatmeal instead of rolled oats.*
- *Use ground mixed spice or ginger instead of cinnamon.*
- *Use pears instead of apples.*
- *Use unsweetened apple juice instead of grape juice.*
- *Use chopped nuts, such as almonds or Brazil nuts, instead of some or all of the oats for a nutty streusel topping.*

freezing instructions

Allow to cool completely, then transfer to a rigid, freezeproof container. Cover, seal and label. Freeze for up to 3 months. Defrost, and reheat in a moderate oven until piping hot.

the exam booster

THIS DELICIOUS AND *nutritious menu from the brain foods section is packed with slow-release carbohydrates and protein that will help to improve concentration. So instead of burning the midnight oil over a pile of books, sit down to this appetising meal the night before an exam.*

asparagus *with* hazelnuts

A boron-rich starter – all the better to improve mental alertness.

ingredients

- 450g (1lb) asparagus, trimmed
- 25–55g (1–2oz) toasted hazelnuts, roughly chopped
- fresh coriander sprigs, to garnish

for the dressing

- 2tbsp hazelnut oil
- 1tbsp olive oil
- 1tbsp lemon juice
- 1tbsp honey
- 1tsp Dijon mustard
- 2 spring onions, finely chopped
- 1 clove garlic, crushed
- 1tbsp chopped fresh coriander
- sea salt
- freshly ground black pepper

serves ***four***
preparation time ***10 minutes***
cooking time ***8–12 minutes***

method

1 Tie the asparagus in small bundles and cook upright in a deep saucepan of lightly salted, boiling water for 8–12 minutes, until tender. Ensure that the tips are above the water so that they are steamed rather than boiled.
2 To make the dressing, put the oils, lemon juice, honey, mustard, spring onions, garlic, chopped coriander and seasoning in a bowl and whisk together.
3 Drain the asparagus, untie the bundles and divide the stalks between four serving plates.
4 Drizzle the dressing over the asparagus, scatter some hazelnuts over each portion and garnish with the coriander sprigs.
5 Serve immediately with crusty wholemeal bread.

poached salmon *with* celery sauce

Salmon is a valuable source of omega-3 fatty acids – brain-boosting essentials and important for the healthy growth and repair of cells.

ingredients

- 6 salmon steaks, each weighing about 175g (6oz)
- vegetable stock (see recipe on page 20), for poaching
- fresh parsley sprigs, to garnish

for the sauce

- 25g (1oz) butter
- 3 shallots (French shallots), finely chopped
- 4 sticks celery, finely chopped
- 2tbsp cornflour
- 350ml (12fl oz) milk
- 2tbsp chopped fresh parsley
- sea salt
- freshly ground black pepper

serves *six*
preparation time *10 minutes*
cooking time *15–20 minutes*

method

1 Place the salmon steaks in a large, deep frying pan and pour over enough stock to cover the fish completely. Cover, bring to the boil, then reduce the heat and simmer gently for about 10 minutes, until the salmon is cooked and the flesh just flakes when tested with a fork.

2 Meanwhile, melt the butter in a saucepan. Add the shallots and celery, cover and cook for 15–20 minutes, until the vegetables are tender, stirring occasionally.

3 Blend the cornflour with a little of the milk, then stir in the remaining milk. Bring to the boil, stirring continuously, until the sauce comes to the boil and thickens. Simmer gently for 2 minutes, stirring continuously.

4 Stir in the hot cooked vegetables and chopped parsley. Season to taste.

5 Using a slotted spoon or fish slice, carefully remove the salmon steaks from the stock and place on warmed serving plates. Discard the stock.

6 Spoon some celery sauce over the fish, or alongside, and garnish with the parsley sprigs.

7 Serve with cooked fresh vegetables, such as new potatoes, carrots and broccoli.

blackberry *and* apple streusel

The oats in this dessert provide brain-nourishing B vitamins, and the apples and blackberries are good sources of vitamin C.

ingredients

- 115g (4oz) plain wholemeal flour
- 115g (4oz) light brown sugar
- 115g (4oz) butter, chopped
- 55g (2oz) rolled oats
- 1tsp ground cinnamon
- 350g (12oz) ripe blackberries
- 450g (1lb) eating apples (peeled and cored weight), thinly sliced
- finely grated rind of 1 lemon
- 2tbsp unsweetened red grape juice
- 2tbsp honey

serves *four to six*
preparation time *15 minutes*
cooking time *30 minutes*

method

1 Preheat the oven to 190°C/375°F/gas mark 5.

2 Put the flour and sugar in a bowl and lightly rub in the chopped butter until the mixture resembles coarse crumbs. Stir in the oats and ground cinnamon.

3 Put the blackberries, apples and lemon rind in an ovenproof dish and stir.

4 Mix together the grape juice and honey and pour over the fruit.

5 Spoon the oat streusel mixture evenly over the fruit.

6 Bake for about 30 minutes, or until the fruit is cooked and the streusel topping is golden brown and crunchy.

7 Serve hot or cold with home-made custard or plain yoghurt.

memory *foods*

THE B GROUP VITAMINS are essential for brain function – a lack of them is known to affect mental processing, perception, judgement, memory and reasoning. Good sources of B vitamins are broccoli, asparagus, dark-green leafy vegetables such as spinach, bananas, avocados, root vegetables, pulses, nuts, brown rice, eggs, poultry, meat, dairy products, liver and fish. Oily fish also contain omega-3 essential fatty acids, which are an important component of brain cell membranes. Zinc is needed by the brain for mental alertness, memory, recall and concentration. Good sources of zinc are pulses, wholegrain bread and cereals, and fish.

guacamole *with* vegetable crudités

Guacamole is quick and easy to make for a popular starter or snack served with fresh vegetable crudités. Avocados contain B vitamins and essential fatty acids, which are important for maintaining healthy brain tissue and memory.

ingredients

- 2 ripe avocados
- juice of 1 small lime
- 3 shallots (French shallots), finely chopped
- 2 plum (Roma) tomatoes, skinned, seeded and finely chopped
- 1 fresh green chilli, seeded and finely chopped
- 1 clove garlic, crushed
- 1tbsp chopped fresh coriander
- sea salt
- freshly ground black pepper
- fresh coriander sprigs, to garnish
- prepared vegetable crudités, including carrot, cucumber and pepper (capsicum) sticks, baby sweetcorn, cauliflower florets, cherry tomatoes and spring onions

serves *four to six*
preparation time *10 minutes*

method

1 Peel and stone the avocados and put the flesh in a bowl. Mash the avocado flesh with the lime juice until smooth.

2 Stir in the shallots, tomatoes, chilli, garlic, chopped coriander and seasoning.

3 Transfer the mixture to a serving dish, garnish with the coriander sprigs and serve immediately with a selection of vegetable crudités alongside.

variations

- *Use lemon juice instead of lime.*
- *Use standard tomatoes instead of plum tomatoes.*
- *Use chopped fresh parsley instead of coriander.*

liver *and* brandy paté

Served with fresh toast, oatcakes or crispbread, this tasty liver paté makes a tempting starter or snack. Liver is a good source of B vitamins, which are essential for a healthy brain and memory.

ingredients

- 1tbsp olive oil
- 1 small onion, chopped
- 1 clove garlic, crushed
- 350g (12oz) lamb's liver, cut into thin strips
- 3tbsp crème fraîche or light sour cream
- 2tbsp brandy
- 1tbsp tomato purée (paste)
- 2tbsp chopped fresh flatleaf parsley
- sea salt
- freshly ground black pepper
- fresh parsley sprigs, to garnish

serves *six*
preparation time *15 minutes, plus chilling time*
cooking time *10 minutes*

method

1 Heat the oil in a non-stick saucepan. Add the onion and garlic, and cook for 5 minutes, stirring occasionally.
2 Add the liver and cook for about 5 minutes, until cooked and tender, stirring frequently.
3 Remove the pan from the heat, cool slightly, then stir in the crème fraîche or light sour cream, brandy, tomato purée, chopped parsley and seasoning.
4 Put the mixture in a blender or food processor and blend until smooth. Transfer to a serving dish, cool, then cover and chill in the refrigerator before serving.
5 Garnish with the parsley sprigs and serve with wholemeal toast, oatcakes or crispbread.

variations

- *Use port instead of brandy.*
- *Use 3 shallots (French shallots) instead of the onion.*

baked eggs *with* mushrooms

Eggs, lightly oven-baked in a nest of vegetables, make a tasty starter or snack. Eggs are a source of B vitamins and zinc, which are nutrients needed by the brain for memory and recall.

ingredients

- 1tbsp olive oil
- 115g (4oz) mushrooms, finely chopped
- 1 small courgette (zucchini), finely chopped
- 1 small yellow pepper (capsicum), seeded and finely chopped
- 1 plum (Roma) tomato, seeded and finely chopped
- 1 clove garlic, crushed
- 1tbsp chopped fresh chives
- sea salt
- freshly ground black pepper
- 4 medium eggs
- fresh chives, to garnish

serves ***four***
preparation time *20 minutes*
cooking time *10–15 minutes*

method

1 Preheat the oven to 180°C/350°F/gas mark 4.
2 Heat the oil in a saucepan and add the mushrooms, courgette, pepper, tomato and garlic. Cover and cook for about 10 minutes, until the vegetables are cooked and tender, stirring occasionally.
3 Drain off and discard the excess juices, then stir in the chives and season to taste.
4 Spoon some of the vegetable mixture into four ramekins or small ovenproof glass dishes and make a well in the centre of each.
5 Break an egg into the centre of each vegetable 'nest', cover the top of the dishes with foil and place the dishes in a shallow baking tin.
6 Pour in enough hot water to come halfway up the sides of the dishes. Bake for 10–15 minutes, until the eggs are cooked and set.
7 Garnish with the chives and serve immediately with wholemeal bread rolls.

variations

- *Use 1 red or green pepper instead of yellow pepper.*
- *Use chopped fresh mixed herbs or parsley instead of chives.*

fish baked *with* lime *and* coriander

White fish fillets are delicious baked with lime and fresh coriander. Fish contains B vitamins and an amino acid called tyrosine, both of which are important for the memory and for healthy brain function.

ingredients

- 4 firm white fish fillets, such as haddock or gemfish, each weighing about 175g (6oz)
- juice of 2 limes
- 2tsp finely grated lime rind
- 2–3tbsp chopped fresh coriander
- sea salt
- freshly ground black pepper
- 15g (½oz) butter
- fresh coriander sprigs, to garnish

serves *four*
preparation time *10 minutes*
cooking time *20–30 minutes*

method

1 Preheat the oven to 180°C/350°F/gas mark 4.

2 Put the fish fillets in a shallow ovenproof dish. Drizzle the lime juice over the fish and sprinkle the lime rind, chopped coriander and seasoning over the top. Dot each fish fillet with a little butter.

3 Cover and bake for 20–30 minutes, until the fish is cooked and the flesh just flakes when tested with a fork.

4 Put the fish fillets on warmed serving plates and garnish with the coriander sprigs.

5 Serve with cooked fresh vegetables, such as mangetout (snowpeas) and swede.

variations

- *Use lemons instead of limes.*
- *Use chopped fresh parsley or mixed herbs instead of coriander.*
- *Use fresh salmon or tuna steaks instead of white fish.*

grilled sardines *with* watercress mayonnaise

Fresh sardines, grilled and served with watercress mayonnaise, make a delicious lunch or snack. Oily fish are a good source of essential fatty acids and zinc, both of which are needed for the production of brain cells.

ingredients

- 700g (1lb 9oz) large sardines, gutted and cleaned
- 1tbsp olive oil
- juice of 1 small lemon
- 1–2tbsp chopped fresh mixed herbs
- small fresh watercress sprigs, to garnish

for the mayonnaise

- 8tbsp mayonnaise (see recipe on page 21)
- 55g (2oz) watercress, finely chopped
- ½tsp freshly grated hot horseradish
- sea salt
- freshly ground black pepper

serves *four*
preparation time *15 minutes*
cooking time *8–14 minutes*

method

1 Put the mayonnaise, chopped watercress and horseradish in a small bowl and mix well. Season to taste with salt and pepper, then cover and set aside.

2 Cover a grill rack with foil and preheat the grill to high. Place the sardines on the rack.

3 Put the oil, lemon juice and chopped herbs in a bowl. Season and mix thoroughly. Lightly brush the sardines all over with the oil mixture.

4 Grill the sardines for about 4–7 minutes on each side, until they are cooked, turning once.

5 Serve the hot sardines with the watercress mayonnaise spooned alongside. Garnish the watercress sprigs.

6 Serve with wholemeal bread and a tomato, pepper (capsicum) and onion salad.

variations

- *Use small mackerel or other small oily fish instead of sardines.*
- *Use chopped fresh parsley instead of mixed herbs.*
- *Use fresh lime juice instead of lemon juice.*

stir-fried lamb *with* garlic *and* ginger

This nutritious stir-fry is quick and easy to prepare. The protein contained in lamb encourages the production of brain-stimulating chemicals. Sunflower and pumpkin seeds contain zinc, which can boost mental alertness.

ingredients

- 115g (4oz) small broccoli florets
- 1tbsp olive oil
- 350g (12oz) lean lamb, cut into thin strips
- 2 cloves garlic, crushed
- 4cm (1½in) piece of fresh root ginger, peeled and finely chopped
- 2 leeks, washed and thinly sliced
- 2 carrots, thinly sliced
- 1 red pepper (capsicum), seeded and sliced
- 85g (3oz) mangetout (snowpeas)
- 85g (3oz) beansprouts
- 2tbsp apple juice
- 2tbsp light soy sauce
- freshly ground black pepper
- 1–2tbsp sunflower or pumpkin seeds

serves ***four***
preparation time *20 minutes*
cooking time *8–10 minutes*

method

1 Blanch the broccoli florets in boiling water for 2 minutes. Drain thoroughly and set aside.
2 Heat the oil in a non-stick wok or large frying pan. Add the lamb, garlic and ginger, and stir-fry over a high heat for about 2 minutes, until the lamb is sealed all over.
3 Add the broccoli, leeks, carrots and red pepper, and stir-fry for 2–3 minutes. Add the mangetout and beansprouts, and stir-fry for another 2–3 minutes.
4 Add the apple juice, soy sauce and black pepper, and stir-fry until the mixture is piping hot and the lamb and vegetables are cooked and tender.
5 Scatter over the sunflower or pumpkin seeds, and serve with brown rice or pasta.

variations

- *The juices can be thickened before serving. Blend 1tsp cornflour with 1tbsp water, add to the juices in the pan and stir-fry until cooked and thickened.*
- *Use cauliflower instead of broccoli.*
- *Use skinless chicken or turkey breast instead of lamb.*

chicken *and* chickpea casserole

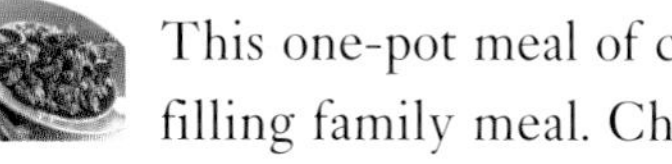

This one-pot meal of chicken, chickpeas and vegetables makes a nutritious and filling family meal. Chickpeas are a good source of zinc, a nutrient needed by the brain for memory and recall.

ingredients

- 1tbsp olive oil
- 450g (1lb) skinless, boneless chicken breast, cut into 2.5cm (1in) cubes
- 225g (8oz) shallots (French shallots), sliced
- 2 leeks, washed and sliced
- 1 green pepper (capsicum), seeded and diced
- 225g (8oz) mushrooms, sliced
- 175g (6oz) frozen peas
- 2 x 400g (14oz) cans chickpeas, rinsed and drained
- 400g (14oz) can tomatoes, chopped
- 1tbsp sun-dried tomato purée (paste)
- 150ml (¼ pint) chicken stock (see recipe on page 20)
- 300ml (½ pint) dry white wine
- 1 bouquet garni
- sea salt
- freshly ground black pepper
- 1tbsp cornflour (optional)
- fresh herb sprigs, to garnish

serves *six*
preparation time *25 minutes*
cooking time *1 hour*

method

1 Preheat the oven to 180°C/350°F/gas mark 4.

2 Heat the oil in a large flameproof, ovenproof casserole dish. Add the chicken pieces and cook gently until sealed all over, stirring occasionally.

3 Stir in the shallots, leeks, green pepper, mushrooms, peas and chickpeas.

4 Add the tomatoes, tomato purée, stock, wine, bouquet garni and seasoning, and stir.

5 Bring to the boil, stirring occasionally, then cover and bake for about 1 hour, until the chicken and vegetables are cooked and tender, stirring once or twice. Remove from the oven and discard the bouquet garni.

6 Blend the cornflour, if using, with 3tbsp water and stir into the casserole. Heat gently, stirring continuously, until the mixture comes to the boil and thickens slightly. Simmer gently for 2 minutes, stirring constantly.

7 Spoon onto warmed serving plates, garnish with herb sprigs and serve with wholemeal bread.

variations

- *Use skinless, boneless turkey breast instead of chicken.*
- *Use canned red kidney beans or flageolet beans instead of chickpeas.*
- *Use red wine instead of white wine.*
- *Use 1 onion instead of shallots.*

freezing instructions

Allow to cool completely, then transfer to a rigid, freezeproof container. Cover, seal and label. Freeze for up to 3 months. Defrost completely, then reheat gently in a saucepan or moderate oven until piping hot.

onion tartlets

These tartlets can be served warm or cold with baked potatoes and a salad. The cold-pressed extra virgin olive oil contains essential fatty acids, which are important for healthy brain tissue and memory function.

ingredients

- 1tbsp olive oil
- 1 large onion, thinly sliced
- 55g (2oz) Cheddar cheese, grated
- 2 medium eggs
- 100ml (3½fl oz) milk
- 1tbsp chopped fresh mixed herbs
- sea salt
- freshly ground black pepper
- fresh herb sprigs, to garnish

for the pastry

- 175g (6oz) plain wholemeal flour
- pinch of salt
- 85g (3oz) butter, chopped

makes *6*
preparation time *35 minutes, plus 30 minutes chilling time*
cooking time *20–30 minutes*

method

1 Preheat the oven to 200°C/400°F/gas mark 6.

2 To make the pastry, put the flour and a pinch of salt in a bowl, then lightly rub in the chopped butter until the mixture resembles breadcrumbs. Add enough cold water to form a soft dough.

3 Roll the dough out on a lightly floured surface and use to line six individual 10cm (4in) fluted flan tins. Refrigerate for 30 minutes.

4 Heat the oil in a frying pan, add the onion and cook for about 10 minutes, until softened, stirring occasionally. Remove from the heat and set aside.

5 Line the pastry cases with non-stick baking paper and fill with baking beans. Place on two baking trays and bake blind for about 10 minutes, until firm and lightly brown. Remove from the oven and lift out the paper and beans. Reduce the oven temperature to 180°C/350°F/gas mark 4.

6 Spoon some cooked onions over the base of each pastry case and sprinkle the cheese over the top. Beat the eggs, milk, chopped herbs and seasoning together and pour into the flan cases over the onions and cheese.

7 Bake for 20–30 minutes, until golden brown.

8 Garnish with the herb sprigs and serve warm or cold with oven-baked potatoes and a mixed salad.

variations

- *Use chopped fresh chives instead of mixed herbs.*
- *Use fresh Parmesan cheese instead of Cheddar cheese.*

freezing instructions

Allow to cool completely, then wrap in foil or seal in a freezer bag and label. Freeze for up to 3 months. Defrost, and serve cold or reheat in a moderate oven until piping hot.

lentil moussaka

This appetising meat-free moussaka is good served with oven-baked potatoes and cooked vegetables. Lentils provide B vitamins and zinc.

ingredients

- 450g (1lb) aubergines (eggplants), sliced
- sea salt
- freshly ground black pepper
- 4tbsp olive oil
- 1 onion, sliced
- 1 red pepper (capsicum), seeded and diced
- 2 leeks, washed and sliced
- 1 clove garlic, crushed
- 450g (1lb) cooked green or brown lentils
- 400g (14oz) can tomatoes, chopped
- 6tbsp red wine
- 1tbsp sun-dried tomato purée (paste)
- 2tsp dried *herbes de provence*
- 350g (12oz) plain yoghurt
- 2 medium eggs
- 25–55g (1–2oz) fresh Parmesan or Cheddar cheese, finely grated (optional)
- fresh herb sprigs, to garnish

serves *four to six*
preparation time *35 minutes, plus 30 minutes' standing time for the aubergines*
cooking time *45 minutes*

method

1 Preheat the oven to 180°C/350°F/gas mark 4.
2 Put the aubergine in a colander, sprinkle with salt and leave for 30 minutes. Rinse well and pat dry.
3 Heat 1tbsp oil in a saucepan, add the onion, red pepper, leeks and garlic. Cook for 5 minutes, stirring occasionally.
4 Add the lentils, tomatoes, red wine, tomato purée, dried herbs and seasoning. Cover, bring to the boil, then reduce the heat and simmer for 10 minutes.
5 Heat the remaining oil and fry the aubergine slices until browned.
6 Put layers of the lentil mixture and aubergines in an ovenproof dish. Beat the yoghurt, eggs and seasoning together and pour over. Sprinkle with cheese. Bake in the oven for about 45 minutes.
7 Garnish with the herb sprigs and serve with baked potatoes and broccoli.

variations

- *Use apple juice instead of red wine.*
- *Use sliced courgettes (zucchini) instead of aubergines.*

sweet *and* sour bean tacos

These generously filled tacos are sure to be a popular choice with family and friends. Beans provide protein, B vitamins and zinc.

ingredients

- 1tbsp cornflour
- 8tbsp unsweetened pineapple juice
- 2tbsp light soy sauce
- 2tbsp light brown sugar
- 2tbsp tomato purée (paste)
- 2tbsp dry sherry
- 2tbsp cider vinegar
- 400g (14oz) can red kidney beans, rinsed and drained
- 400g (14oz) can black-eye beans, rinsed and drained
- 3 plum (Roma) tomatoes, skinned, seeded and chopped
- 6–8 spring onions, chopped
- 1–2tbsp chopped fresh coriander (optional)
- sea salt
- freshly ground black pepper
- 8 taco shells
- grated Cheddar cheese, to serve

serves *four (two tacos each)*
preparation time *10 minutes*
cooking time *15–20 minutes*

method

1 Preheat the oven to 180°C/350°F/gas mark 4.
2 Blend the cornflour with the pineapple juice in a saucepan, then add the soy sauce, sugar, tomato purée, sherry and vinegar, and stir.
3 Heat gently until the sauce comes to the boil and thickens, stirring occasionally. Add the beans, tomatoes and spring onions. Return to the boil, reduce the heat and simmer for 10 minutes, stirring occasionally.
4 Stir in the chopped coriander, if using, and season to taste.
5 Put the tacos on a baking sheet and heat in the oven for 2–3 minutes, until warm.
6 Fill each taco with bean mixture and top with grated cheese. Serve with a mixed dark-green leaf salad.

variations

- *Serve the bean mixture with baked potatoes, brown rice or pasta instead of tacos.*
- *Use chopped fresh mixed herbs or parsley instead of coriander.*

pineapple tarte tatin

This pineapple tart is a real treat, a delicious end to any meal. Almonds contain calcium, magnesium, boron and essential fatty acids, all of which are good for healthy brain function and good memory.

ingredients

- 5tbsp honey
- finely grated rind of 1 lemon
- 900g (2lb) pineapple, peeled, cored and sliced or chopped (approx 550g/1lb 4oz prepared fruit)
- 25g (1oz) flaked almonds, toasted, to decorate

for the pastry

- 175g (6oz) plain wholemeal flour
- 85g (3oz) butter, chopped
- 25g (1oz) sugar
- 1 medium egg yolk

serves *six*
preparation time *25 minutes*
cooking time *25–30 minutes*

method

1 Preheat the oven to 200°C/400°F/gas mark 6.
2 Lightly grease a shallow, 23cm (9in), round non-stick cake tin and set aside.
3 Put the flour in a bowl, then lightly rub in the butter until the mixture resembles breadcrumbs. Stir in the sugar, then add the egg yolk and enough cold water to form a soft dough. Set aside.
4 Warm the honey in a saucepan, then pour it over the bottom of the tin. Sprinkle the lemon rind over the honey. Arrange the pineapple decoratively in overlapping circles in the honey, covering the base completely.
5 Roll the pastry out on a lightly floured surface to a round slightly larger than the tin. Lay the pastry over the pineapple, tucking the excess pastry down the side.
6 Bake for 25–30 minutes, until the pastry is crisp and lightly browned.
7 Place a serving plate on top of the tin, invert and remove the tin. Scatter the pineapple with flaked almonds.
8 Serve warm or cold, with a little plain yoghurt, crème fraîche or light sour cream.

variations

- *Use sliced eating apples or apricots instead of pineapple.*
- *Omit the lemon rind, if preferred.*
- *Use pineapple canned in fruit juice and drained, instead of fresh.*
- *Use the grated rind of 1 small orange instead of the lemon rind.*

grilled fruit *with* yoghurt

Fresh fruits lightly grilled and served with plain yoghurt make a quick and easy dessert. Yoghurt contains substances that keep the brain alert.

ingredients

- 4 apricots
- 2 peaches
- 1 apple
- 1 pear
- 2 bananas
- 3tbsp honey
- 2tbsp unsweetened apple juice
- 1tbsp brandy
- 1–2tsp ground cinnamon
- plain yoghurt, to serve

serves *four*
preparation time *15 minutes*
cooking time *4–6 minutes*

method

1 Dip the apricots and peaches in a large saucepan of boiling water for 15 seconds. Remove with a slotted spoon and plunge into a bowl of cold water. Drain, then peel off the skins.

2 Cover a grill rack with foil and preheat the grill to high. Halve and stone the apricots, stone and thickly slice the peaches, and put them on the grill rack.

3 Peel, core and thinly slice the apple and pear. Peel and slice the bananas diagonally. Add to the other fruit on the grill rack.

4 Put the honey, apple juice, brandy and cinnamon in a small bowl and stir. Drizzle the mixture evenly over the fruit.

5 Grill the fruit for about 4–6 minutes, until hot or cooked to your liking, turning once or twice.

6 Serve hot with some plain yoghurt spooned alongside.

variations

- *Use maple syrup instead of honey.*
- *Use unsweetened orange juice or white grape juice instead of apple.*
- *Use rum instead of brandy.*
- *Use ground ginger or mixed spice instead of cinnamon.*

carrot *and* walnut cake

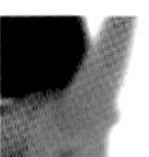

This delicious cake is sure to be a favourite. Carrots and walnuts contain B vitamins, which are essential for mental alertness and memory.

ingredients

- 175g (6oz) butter, softened
- 175g (6oz) light brown sugar
- 3 medium eggs, beaten
- 175g (6oz) plain wholemeal flour
- 55g (2oz) fine oatmeal
- 10ml (2tsp) baking powder
- 225g (8oz) carrots, grated
- 140g (5oz) walnuts, chopped
- 115g (4oz) sultanas
- about 2tbsp milk

for the topping

- 225g (8oz) curd (cottage) cheese
- 1–2tbsp honey
- 1tsp finely grated orange rind

serves *ten*
preparation time *20 minutes*
cooking time *1–1¼ hours*

method

1 Preheat the oven to 180°C/350°F/gas mark 4.

2 Grease and line a deep, 20cm (8in) round cake tin.

3 Cream the butter and sugar in a bowl until light and fluffy. Gradually beat in the eggs, beating well after each addition.

4 Fold in the flour, oatmeal and baking powder, then fold in the carrots, 115g (4oz) walnuts, sultanas and a little milk to give a fairly soft dropping consistency.

5 Transfer the mixture to the cake tin and hollow the centre slightly. Bake for 1–1¼ hours until risen and firm to the touch.

6 Cool in the tin for a few minutes, then turn out on to a wire rack. Remove the lining paper and leave to cool completely.

7 To make the topping, fold the curd cheese, honey and orange rind together, adding honey to taste. Spread over the top of the cold cake and sprinkle the remaining walnuts over the top.

8 Store the cake in the refrigerator.

variations

- *Omit the curd cheese topping and serve the cake plain.*
- *Use pecan nuts instead of walnuts.*
- *Use raisins or chopped dried apricots instead of sultanas.*

freezing instructions

Allow to cool completely (step 6), then wrap in foil or seal in a freezer bag and label. Freeze for up to 3 months. Defrost for several hours at room temperature, then make the topping (step 7) and serve.

you *must* remember this

PACKED FULL OF PROTEIN *and B group vitamins, as well as the minerals zinc, magnesium, boron and selenium that are vital for brain function, this unforgettable selection of nutritious recipes from the memory foods section can help to improve mental alertness and memory.*

guacamole *with* vegetable crudités

Avocado is rich in the B vitamins – essential for brain function and quick recall.

ingredients

- 2 ripe avocados
- juice of 1 small lime
- 3 shallots (French shallots), finely chopped
- 2 plum (Roma) tomatoes, skinned, seeded and finely chopped
- 1 fresh green chilli, seeded and finely chopped
- 1 clove garlic, crushed
- 1tbsp chopped fresh coriander
- sea salt
- freshly ground black pepper
- fresh coriander sprigs, to garnish
- prepared vegetable crudités, including carrot, cucumber and pepper (capsicum) sticks, baby sweetcorn, cauliflower florets, cherry tomatoes and spring onions

serves *four to six*
preparation time *10 minutes*

method

1 Peel and stone the avocados and put the flesh in a bowl. Mash the avocado flesh with the lime juice until smooth.
2 Stir in the shallots, tomatoes, chilli, garlic, chopped coriander and seasoning.
3 Transfer the mixture to a serving dish, garnish with the coriander sprigs and serve immediately with a selection of vegetable crudités alongside.

chicken *and* chickpea casserole

The chickpeas in this dish are a valuable source of zinc, and the chicken is rich in protein – both excellent brain nutrients.

ingredients

- 1tbsp olive oil
- 450g (1lb) skinless, boneless chicken breast, cut into 2.5cm (1in) cubes
- 225g (8oz) shallots (French shallots), sliced
- 2 leeks, washed and sliced
- 1 green pepper (capsicum), seeded and diced
- 225g (8oz) mushrooms, sliced
- 175g (6oz) frozen peas
- 2 x 400g (14oz) cans chickpeas, rinsed and drained
- 400g (14oz) can tomatoes, chopped
- 1tbsp sun-dried tomato purée (paste)
- 150ml (¼ pint) chicken stock (see recipe on page 20)
- 300ml (½ pint) dry white wine
- 1 bouquet garni
- sea salt
- freshly ground black pepper
- 1tbsp cornflour (optional)
- fresh herb sprigs, to garnish

serves *six*
preparation time *25 minutes*
cooking time *1 hour*

method

1 Preheat the oven to 180°C/350°F/gas mark 4.
2 Heat the oil in a large flameproof, ovenproof casserole dish. Add the chicken pieces and cook gently until sealed all over, stirring occasionally.
3 Stir in the shallots, leeks, green pepper, mushrooms, peas and chickpeas.
4 Add the tomatoes, tomato purée, stock, wine, bouquet garni and seasoning and stir.
5 Bring to the boil, stirring occasionally, then cover and bake for about 1 hour, until the chicken and vegetables are cooked and tender, stirring once or twice. Remove from the oven and discard the bouquet garni.
6 Blend the cornflour, if using, with 3tbsp water and stir into the casserole. Heat gently, stirring continuously, until the mixture comes to the boil and thickens slightly. Simmer gently for 2 minutes, stirring occasionally.
7 Spoon on to warmed serving plates, garnish with herb sprigs and serve with wholemeal bread.

pineapple tarte tatin

Almonds make this dessert rich in calcium, magnesium, boron and essential fatty acids – great for memory and brain function.

ingredients

- 5tbsp honey
- finely grated rind of 1 lemon
- 900g (2lb) pineapple, peeled, cored and sliced or chopped (approx 550g/1lb 4oz prepared fruit)
- 25g (1oz) flaked almonds, toasted, to decorate

for the pastry

- 175g (6oz) plain wholemeal flour
- 85g (3oz) butter, chopped
- 25g (1oz) sugar
- 1 medium egg yolk

serves *six*
preparation time *25 minutes*
cooking time *25–30 minutes*

method

1 Preheat the oven to 200°C/400°F/gas mark 6.
2 Lightly grease a shallow, 23cm (9in), round non-stick cake tin and set aside.
3 Put the flour in a bowl, then lightly rub in the butter until the mixture resembles breadcrumbs. Stir in the sugar, then add the egg yolk and enough cold water to form a soft dough. Set aside.
4 Warm the honey in a saucepan, then pour it over the bottom of the tin. Sprinkle the lemon rind over the honey. Arrange the pineapple decoratively in overlapping circles in the honey, covering the base completely.
5 Roll the pastry out on a lightly floured surface to a round slightly larger than the tin. Lay the pastry over the pineapple, tucking the excess pastry down the side.
6 Bake for 25–30 minutes, until the pastry is crisp and lightly browned.
7 Place a serving plate on top of the tin, invert and remove the tin. Scatter the pineapple with flaked almonds.
8 Serve warm or cold with a little plain yoghurt, crème fraîche or light sour cream.

focus *foods*

MINERALS ARE IMPORTANT *for healthy brain function. Zinc is needed for mental alertness and concentration – good sources are pulses, wholegrain bread and cereals, and fish. The trace element boron is needed in only tiny amounts but is essential for mental alertness. Boron is found in fresh and dried fruits, green vegetables, walnuts, almonds and hazelnuts. A deficiency of iron may affect thinking in some people. Iron-rich foods include red meats, dark-meat poultry, lamb's liver and kidneys, green leafy vegetables, nuts, dried fruits, wholegrains, enriched breads and cereals, and fish.*

butternut squash *and* leek soup

This mildly spiced soup is ideal for chilly days. Squash provides beta carotene, plus B vitamins and iron, essential for concentration.

ingredients

- 1tbsp olive oil
- 1 onion, chopped
- 2 leeks, washed and thinly sliced
- 1 clove garlic, crushed
- 2tsp ground coriander
- 2tsp ground cumin
- 450g (1lb) diced butternut squash (pumpkin) – peeled and seeded weight
- 850ml (1½pints) vegetable stock (see recipe on page 20)
- sea salt
- freshly ground black pepper
- fresh herb sprigs, to garnish

serves *four*
preparation time *15 minutes*
cooking time *30 minutes*

method

1 Heat the oil in a large saucepan. Add the onion, leeks and garlic, and cook gently for 3 minutes.
2 Add the ground spices and cook for 1 minute, stirring.
3 Stir in the squash, stock and seasoning. Cover, bring to the boil, then reduce the heat and simmer for about 20 minutes, until the vegetables are cooked and tender, stirring occasionally.
4 Remove the pan from the heat and set aside to cool slightly, then purée the soup in a blender or food processor until smooth.
5 Return the soup to the rinsed-out saucepan and reheat until hot, stirring occasionally.
6 Ladle into warmed soup bowls to serve and garnish with the herb sprigs.
7 Serve with wholemeal bread or toast.

variations

- *Use pumpkin flesh instead of butternut squash.*
- *Use 6 shallots (French shallots) instead of the onion.*

freezing instructions

Allow to cool completely, then transfer to a rigid, freezeproof container. Cover, seal and label. Freeze for up to 3 months. Defrost, and reheat gently in a saucepan until piping hot.

minted pea soup

A steaming hot bowl of home-made soup served with wholemeal bread rolls makes an excellent starter for cold winter days. Peas are a good source of zinc, a nutrient needed by the brain for concentration.

ingredients

- 1tbsp olive oil
- 1 onion, chopped
- 2 leeks, washed and sliced
- 450g (1lb) fresh peas (shelled weight)
- 850ml (1½pints) vegetable stock (see recipe on page 20)
- sea salt
- freshly ground black pepper
- 2tbsp chopped fresh mint
- fresh mint sprigs, to garnish

serves *four*
preparation time *10 minutes*
cooking time *25–30 minutes*

method

1 Heat the oil in a large saucepan. Add the onion and leeks and cook gently for 5 minutes, stirring.
2 Stir in the peas, stock and seasoning. Cover, bring to the boil, then reduce the heat and simmer for 15–20 minutes, until the vegetables are tender.
3 Purée the soup in a food processor, then return it to the rinsed-out saucepan, add the chopped mint and reheat.
4 Ladle into soup bowls and garnish with the mint sprigs. Serve with wholemeal rolls.

variations

- *Use frozen peas if fresh peas are not available.*
- *Use mushrooms or courgettes (zucchini) instead of peas.*

freezing instructions

Allow to cool completely, then transfer to a rigid, freezeproof container. Cover, seal and label. Freeze for up to 3 months. Defrost, and reheat gently in a saucepan until piping hot.

flaked tuna *and* chickpea salad

Chickpeas, salad vegetables and flaked tuna with a simple dressing make this a tasty starter. Fish contains the amino acid tyrosine, used to make brain-stimulating chemicals.

ingredients

- 400g (14oz) can chickpeas, rinsed and drained
- 225g (8oz) cherry tomatoes, halved
- 1 red pepper (capsicum), seeded and diced
- half a cucumber, diced
- 115g (4oz) mangetout (snowpeas), chopped
- 200g (7oz) can tuna in water, drained and flaked
- 115g (4oz) mixed salad leaves
- fresh herb sprigs, to garnish

for the dressing

- 4tbsp tomato juice
- 2tbsp olive oil
- 1tsp balsamic vinegar
- 1–2tbsp chopped fresh mixed herbs
- ½tsp sugar
- sea salt
- freshly ground black pepper

serves *six*
preparation time *15 minutes*

method

1 Put the chickpeas, cherry tomatoes, red pepper, cucumber and mangetout in a bowl and mix well.
2 Put the tomato juice, olive oil, vinegar, chopped herbs, sugar and seasoning in a small bowl, and whisk together.
3 Pour the dressing over the vegetables and toss to mix. Add the flaked tuna and stir gently.
4 Arrange the mixed salad leaves on six serving plates and spoon some tuna mixture onto each plate. Garnish with the herb sprigs.
5 Serve with oatcakes, crispbread or wholemeal bread.

variations

- *Use canned salmon or crab instead of tuna.*
- *Use canned black-eye or red kidney beans instead of chickpeas.*

fettuccine *with* mussel sauce

Freshly cooked pasta, topped with a generous serving of tomato and mussel sauce, makes a tasty meal. As a complex carbohydrate, pasta can help to calm an overactive mind and aids concentration.

ingredients

- 1tbsp olive oil
- 4 shallots (French shallots) or 1 small onion, finely chopped
- 1 clove garlic, crushed
- 400g (14oz) can tomatoes, chopped
- 150ml (¼ pint dry) white wine
- 1tbsp tomato purée (paste)
- sea salt
- freshly ground black pepper
- 225g (8oz) fettucine
- 225g (8oz) cooked, shelled small mussels
- 2tbsp chopped fresh flatleaf parsley
- 6–8 cooked fresh mussels in their shells
- fresh flatleaf parsley sprigs, to garnish

serves *two*
preparation time *10 minutes*
cooking time *25 minutes*

method

1 Heat the oil in a saucepan, add the shallots or onion and garlic, and cook for 5 minutes, stirring occasionally, until soft.
2 Stir in the tomatoes, wine, tomato purée and seasoning. Bring to the boil, then simmer, uncovered, for about 15 minutes, until the sauce has thickened, stirring occasionally.
3 Meanwhile, cook the pasta until just cooked or *al dente*.
4 Stir the mussels and chopped parsley into the tomato sauce and cook for about 5 minutes, until piping hot.
5 Drain the pasta thoroughly and place on warmed serving plates. Spoon the mussel sauce over the pasta and garnish with mussels in their shells and the parsley sprigs.
6 Serve with a mixed dark-green leaf salad.

variations

- *Use spaghetti or tagliatelle instead of fettucine.*
- *Use cooked, shelled prawns instead of mussels.*
- *Use red wine instead of white wine.*
- *Add 1 finely chopped, seeded fresh red chilli to the sauce with the tomatoes.*

baked stuffed trout

Baked stuffed trout are delicious served with cooked fresh vegetables. Oily fish such as trout provide essential fatty acids, and enriched oatmeal provides iron, both important nutrients for healthy brain tissue and good concentration.

ingredients

- 1tbsp olive oil
- 1 small onion, finely chopped
- 85g (3oz) fresh shiitake or oyster mushrooms, finely chopped
- 25g (1oz) medium oatmeal
- 25g (1oz) hazelnuts or almonds, finely chopped
- finely grated rind of 1 small lemon
- 1tbsp chopped fresh parsley
- sea salt
- freshly ground black pepper
- 4 rainbow trout, each weighing about 280g (10oz), gutted and cleaned, with heads and tails left on
- juice of 2 lemons
- fresh parsley sprigs, to garnish

serves *four*
preparation time *20 minutes*
cooking time *30–40 minutes*

method

1 Preheat the oven to 180°C/350°F/gas mark 4.

2 Heat the oil in a saucepan, add the onion and mushrooms, and cook for about 5 minutes, until softened, stirring occasionally.

3 Remove the pan from the heat, add the oatmeal, hazelnuts or almonds, lemon rind, chopped parsley and seasoning, and mix well. Spoon some of the oatmeal mixture into each trout.

4 Place the trout side-by-side in a shallow, ovenproof dish and drizzle the lemon juice over the fish.

5 Cover with foil and bake for 30–40 minutes, until the fish is cooked and the flesh just flakes when tested with a fork.

6 Garnish with the parsley sprigs and serve with cooked fresh vegetables, such as new potatoes, green cabbage and carrots.

variations

- *Use mackerel instead of trout.*
- *Use button mushrooms instead of shiitake or oyster mushrooms.*
- *Use Brazil nuts or walnuts instead of hazelnuts or almonds.*

chicken, tomato *and* red wine casserole

This delicious chicken casserole, served with mashed potatoes and cooked fresh vegetables, is a popular family meal. As a high-protein food, chicken is good for stimulating the brain and increasing the ability to focus.

ingredients

- 1tbsp olive oil
- 4 skinless chicken portions (2 leg and 2 breast portions)
- 350g (12oz) baby (pickling) onions
- 4 carrots, sliced
- 2 sticks celery, chopped
- 350g (12oz) baby button mushrooms
- 1 clove garlic, crushed
- 400g (14oz) can tomatoes, chopped
- 300ml (½ pint) red wine
- 150ml (¼ pint) chicken stock (see recipe on page 20)
- 2tsp dried *herbes de provence*
- sea salt
- freshly ground black pepper
- 2tbsp cornflour
- fresh herb sprigs, to garnish

serves *four*
preparation time *15 minutes*
cooking time *1½ hours*

method

1 Preheat the oven to 180°C/350°F/gas mark 4.

2 Heat the oil in a large flameproof, ovenproof casserole dish, add the chicken and cook gently until sealed all over, turning once or twice.

3 Remove the dish from the heat and stir in the onions, carrots, celery, mushrooms, garlic, tomatoes, wine, stock, dried herbs and seasoning.

4 Cover and bake for about 1½ hours, until the chicken and vegetables are cooked and tender, stirring once or twice.

5 Remove from the oven. Using a slotted spoon, remove the chicken from the casserole, place on a warmed plate, cover and keep hot.

6 Blend the cornflour with 4tbsp water and stir into the casserole. Bring to the boil, stirring continuously, until the vegetable sauce thickens slightly. Simmer gently for 2 minutes, stirring.

7 Place the chicken portions on warmed serving plates and spoon some vegetable sauce over. Garnish with the herb sprigs.

8 Serve with mashed potatoes, green beans and parsnips.

variations

- *Use white wine or medium cider instead of red wine.*
- *Use shallots (French shallots) instead of baby onions.*
- *Use parsnips instead of carrots.*

freezing instructions

Allow to cool completely, then transfer to a rigid, freezeproof container. Cover, seal and label. Freeze for up to 3 months. Defrost completely, and reheat in a moderate oven until piping hot.

turkey *with* herbed mustard sauce

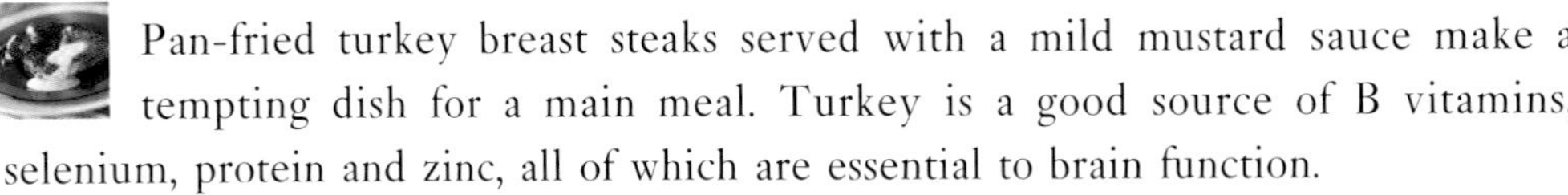

Pan-fried turkey breast steaks served with a mild mustard sauce make a tempting dish for a main meal. Turkey is a good source of B vitamins, selenium, protein and zinc, all of which are essential to brain function.

ingredients

- 1tbsp olive oil
- 15g (½oz) butter
- 4 turkey breast steaks, each weighing about 125g (4½oz)

for the sauce

- 2tbsp cornflour
- 200ml (7fl oz) milk
- 150ml (¼ pint) vegetable stock, cooled (see recipe on page 20)
- 1tbsp wholegrain mustard
- 1tsp dried mixed herbs
- 1tsp honey
- sea salt
- freshly ground black pepper
- fresh herb sprigs, to garnish

serves *four*
preparation time *10 minutes*
cooking time *20 minutes*

method

1 Heat the oil and butter gently in a non-stick frying pan until the butter is melted. Add the turkey breast steaks and cook gently for about 20 minutes, turning once, until cooked, tender and lightly browned all over.
2 Meanwhile, make the mustard sauce. In a saucepan, blend the cornflour with a little of the milk. Stir in the remaining milk and stock, then heat gently, stirring continuously, until the sauce comes to the boil and thickens. Simmer gently for 2 minutes, stirring.
3 Stir in the mustard, dried herbs, honey and seasoning, and heat gently until piping hot, stirring.
4 Serve the turkey steaks with the mustard sauce poured over. Garnish with the herb sprigs.
5 Serve with baked potatoes, grilled peppers (capsicums) and aubergines (eggplants) or courgettes (zucchini).

variations

- *Use chicken breast portions instead of turkey.*
- *Use 1tbsp chopped fresh mixed herbs instead of dried herbs.*
- *Add an extra 1tbsp wholegrain mustard to the sauce for a stronger mustard flavour.*

ratatouille *and* bean pot

The addition of beans to ratatouille adds flavour and texture. Beans are an excellent source of iron, which is an essential nutrient for brain function.

ingredients

- 2 onions, sliced
- 2 cloves garlic, thinly sliced
- 1 aubergine (eggplant), sliced
- 2 courgettes (zucchini), sliced
- 1 each green, red and yellow pepper (capsicum), seeded and sliced
- 400g (14oz) can tomatoes, chopped
- 6tbsp red wine
- 1tbsp tomato purée (paste)
- 2tsp dried *herbes de provence*
- 400g (14oz) can red kidney beans, rinsed and drained
- 400g (14oz) can black-eye beans, rinsed and drained
- sea salt
- freshly ground black pepper
- fresh herb sprigs, to garnish

serves *four to six*
preparation time *15 minutes*
cooking time *1 hour*

method

1 Preheat the oven to 180°C/350°F/gas mark 4.

2 Put all the ingredients, except the herb garnish, in a large ovenproof casserole dish and mix well. Cover and bake for about 1 hour, until the vegetables are cooked and tender, stirring once or twice.

3 Garnish with the herb sprigs and serve hot or cold with crusty wholemeal bread or baked potatoes topped with a little grated Cheddar cheese.

variations

- *Use unsweetened apple juice or medium cider instead of red wine.*
- *Use canned chickpeas and flageolet beans instead of red kidney and black-eye beans.*
- *Add 225g (8oz) baby button mushrooms to the vegetable mixture before cooking.*

freezing instructions

Allow to cool completely, then transfer to a rigid, freezeproof container. Cover, seal and label. Freeze for up to 3 months. Defrost completely, and reheat gently in a saucepan or in a moderate oven until piping hot.

roast new potatoes *with* shallots

This is a delicious way of serving new potatoes. Potatoes are a complex carbohydrate, good for helping you to focus and concentrate.

ingredients

- 450g (1lb) baby new potatoes
- 350g (12oz) small shallots (French shallots)
- 2tbsp olive oil
- sea salt
- freshly ground black pepper
- 1tbsp chopped fresh parsley (optional)
- 1tbsp chopped fresh mint (optional)
- fresh mint sprigs, to garnish

serves ***four*** *as an accompaniment*
preparation time *10 minutes*
cooking time *45–60 minutes*

method

1 Preheat the oven to 200°C/400°F/gas mark 6.
2 Put the potatoes and shallots in a roasting tin, add the oil and seasoning, and toss until the vegetables are coated all over.
3 Bake for 45–60 minutes, until the vegetables are cooked, tender and golden brown, stirring once or twice.
4 Sprinkle over the chopped herbs, if using, and stir. Garnish with the mint sprigs and serve with cooked fresh vegetables, such as chopped spinach and carrots.

variations

- *Use baby (pickling) onions instead of shallots.*
- *Use sesame oil instead of olive oil.*
- *Use chopped fresh mixed herbs instead of the parsley and mint.*

okra *with* spicy tomato sauce

This dish makes a great accompaniment to grilled chicken or fish. Tomatoes provide vitamin C, a nutrient good for a healthy brain.

ingredients

- 700g (1lb 9oz) tomatoes, skinned, seeded and chopped
- 6 shallots (French shallots), thinly sliced
- 1 small leek, washed and thinly sliced
- 2 sticks celery, finely chopped
- 1 clove garlic, crushed
- 150ml (¼ pint) red wine
- 2tbsp sun-dried tomato purée (paste)
- 2tsp ground cumin
- 1tsp ground coriander
- 1tsp hot chilli powder
- sea salt
- freshly ground black pepper
- 700g (1lb 9oz) okra

serves *six*
preparation time *15 minutes*
cooking time *25 minutes*

method

1 Put the tomatoes, shallots, leek, celery, garlic, wine, tomato purée, ground spices and seasoning in a saucepan and mix well.
2 Bring to the boil, then reduce the heat, cover and simmer for about 25 minutes, until the vegetables are tender.
3 Purée the vegetables in a food processor, then return to the rinsed-out saucepan and reheat.
4 Cook the okra in boiling water for about 5 minutes, until tender.
5 Serve the okra with the tomato sauce spooned over, with wholemeal rolls, baked potatoes or brown rice.

variations

- *Serve the spicy tomato sauce with other cooked fresh vegetables, such as baby sweetcorn or baby courgettes (zucchini).*
- *Use 1 onion instead of shallots.*
- *Use unsweetened apple juice or white wine instead of red wine.*

chocolate apple *and* sultana cake

This delicious fruity chocolate cake also makes an ideal dessert served with home-made custard or plain yoghurt. Dried fruit such as sultanas provides iron, magnesium and B vitamins, all good for a healthy brain and nervous system.

ingredients

- 175g (6oz) butter, softened
- 175g (6oz) light brown sugar
- 3 medium eggs, beaten
- 280g (10oz) plain wholemeal flour
- 2tsp baking powder
- 1tsp ground mixed spice
- 3tbsp cocoa powder, sifted
- 350g (12oz) cooking apples, peeled, cored and diced
- 175g (6oz) sultanas
- approx. 6tbsp milk
- 175g (6oz) plain (dark) chocolate, roughly chopped

serves *ten*
preparation time *20 minutes*
cooking time *1¼–1½ hours*

method

1 Preheat the oven to 170°C/325°F/gas mark 3.

2 Grease and line a deep 20cm (8in) round cake tin.

3 Cream the butter and sugar in a bowl until light and fluffy. Gradually beat in the eggs, beating well after each addition.

4 Fold in the flour, baking powder, mixed spice and cocoa powder, then fold in the apples, sultanas and enough milk to give a fairly soft dropping consistency. Fold in the chocolate.

5 Transfer the mixture to the cake tin and level the surface. Bake for 1¼–1½ hours, until risen and firm to the touch.

6 Cool in the tin for a few minutes, then turn out onto a wire rack. Remove the lining paper and leave to cool completely.

7 Serve the apple cake warm or cold with a little home-made custard, plain yoghurt, crème fraîche or light sour cream.

variations

- *Use chopped dried dates or chopped ready-to-eat dried apricots instead of sultanas.*
- *Brush the cake with a little warmed honey or maple syrup and sprinkle with cane sugar just before serving.*

freezing instructions

Allow to cool completely, then wrap in foil or seal in a freezer bag and label. Freeze for up to 3 months. Defrost for several hours at room temperature before serving.

compote *of* winter fruits

Fresh winter fruits soaked in a fruit juice mixture are delicious served with a little plain yoghurt, crème fraîche or light sour cream. Fresh fruit is a good source of vitamin C, a nutrient that helps with the absorption of iron, and both are important nutrients for good brain function.

ingredients

- 200ml (7fl oz) unsweetened apple juice
- 200ml (7fl oz) unsweetened white grape juice
- 2tbsp ginger wine
- 2 cinnamon sticks, broken in half
- 6 whole cloves
- 1 baby pineapple
- 1 medium-sized ripe mango
- 1 star fruit (carambola)
- 175g (6oz) fresh dates
- 1 apple
- 1 pear
- 2 kiwifruit
- fresh mint sprigs, to decorate

serves *six*
preparation time *15 minutes*
cooking time *10 minutes*

method

1 Put the fruit juices, ginger wine, cinnamon sticks and cloves in a saucepan and heat gently until boiling. Remove from the heat.
2 Meanwhile, prepare the fruit. Peel, core and chop the pineapple. Peel, stone and dice the mango. Slice the star fruit (carambola). Stone and chop the dates. Peel, core and slice the apple and pear. Peel and slice the kiwifruit. Put the prepared fruit in a serving bowl and stir.
3 Pour the hot fruit juice mixture over the fruit and stir gently. Set aside to cool, then cover and chill before serving.
4 Remove and discard the cinnamon stick and cloves before serving. Decorate with the mint sprigs and serve with a little plain yoghurt, crème fraîche or light sour cream.

variations

- *Use unsweetened orange juice and pineapple juice instead of the apple and grape juices.*
- *Use a melon instead of pineapple.*
- *Use brandy, rum or fruit liqueur instead of ginger wine.*

quiz *night*

BE QUICK OFF THE *mark on quiz night – this selection of recipes from the focus foods section provides excellent nourishment for your brain and enhances the ability to focus as the recipes contain the B group vitamins as well as other essential nutrients, such as zinc, boron and iron.*

flaked tuna *and* chickpea salad

An excellent source of the amino acid tyrosine, the tuna in this recipe will aid concentration.

ingredients

- 400g (14oz) can chickpeas, rinsed and drained
- 225g (8oz) cherry tomatoes, halved
- 1 red pepper (capsicum), seeded and diced
- half a cucumber, diced
- 115g (4oz) mangetout (snowpeas), chopped
- 200g (7oz) can tuna in water, drained and flaked
- 115g (4oz) mixed salad leaves
- fresh herb sprigs, to garnish

for the dressing

- 4tbsp tomato juice
- 2tbsp olive oil
- 1tsp balsamic vinegar
- 1–2tbsp chopped fresh mixed herbs
- ½tsp sugar
- sea salt
- freshly ground black pepper

serves *six*
preparation time *15 minutes*

method

1 Put the chickpeas, cherry tomatoes, red pepper, cucumber and mangetout in a bowl, and mix well.
2 Put the tomato juice, olive oil, vinegar, chopped herbs, sugar and seasoning in a small bowl, and whisk together.
3 Pour the dressing over the vegetables and toss to mix. Add the flaked tuna and stir gently.
4 Arrange the mixed salad leaves on six serving plates and spoon some tuna mixture on to each plate. Garnish with the herb sprigs.
5 Serve with oatcakes, crispbread or wholemeal bread.

turkey *with* herbed mustard sauce

A succulent all-rounder when it comes to focusing the mind, turkey contains B vitamins, selenium, protein and zinc.

ingredients

- 1tbsp olive oil
- 15g (½oz) butter
- 4 turkey breast steaks, each weighing about 125g (4½oz)

for the sauce

- 2tbsp cornflour
- 200ml (7fl oz) milk
- 150ml (¼ pint) vegetable stock, cooled (see recipe on page 20)
- 1tbsp wholegrain mustard
- 1tsp dried mixed herbs
- 1tsp honey
- sea salt
- freshly ground black pepper
- fresh herb sprigs, to garnish

serves *four*
preparation time *10 minutes*
cooking time *20 minutes*

method

1 Heat the oil and butter gently in a non-stick frying pan until the butter is melted. Add the turkey breast steaks and cook gently for about 20 minutes, turning once, until cooked, tender and lightly browned all over.

2 Meanwhile, make the mustard sauce. In a saucepan, blend the cornflour with a little of the milk. Stir in the remaining milk and stock, then heat gently, stirring continuously, until the sauce comes to the boil and thickens. Simmer gently for 2 minutes, stirring.

3 Stir in the mustard, dried herbs, honey and seasoning, and heat gently until piping hot, stirring.

4 Serve the turkey steaks with the mustard sauce poured over. Garnish with the herb sprigs.

5 Serve with baked potatoes, grilled peppers (capsicums) and aubergines (eggplants) or courgettes (zucchini).

compote *of* winter fruits

A juicy way to round off this mind-strengthening menu – most fresh fruits provide plenty of vitamin C.

ingredients

- 200ml (7fl oz) unsweetened apple juice
- 200ml (7fl oz) unsweetened white grape juice
- 2tbsp ginger wine
- 2 cinnamon sticks, broken in half
- 6 whole cloves
- 1 baby pineapple
- 1 medium-sized ripe mango
- 1 star fruit (carambola)
- 175g (6oz) fresh dates
- 1 apple
- 1 pear
- 2 kiwifruit
- fresh mint sprigs, to decorate

serves *six*
preparation time *15 minutes*
cooking time *10 minutes*

method

1 Put the fruit juices, ginger wine, cinnamon sticks and cloves in a saucepan and heat gently until boiling. Remove from the heat.

2 Meanwhile, prepare the fruit. Peel, core and chop the pineapple. Peel, stone and dice the mango. Slice the star fruit (carambola). Stone and chop the dates. Peel, core and slice the apple and pear. Peel and slice the kiwifruit. Put the prepared fruit in a serving bowl and stir.

3 Pour the hot fruit juice mixture over the fruit and stir gently. Set aside to cool, then cover and chill before serving.

4 Remove and discard the cinnamon stick and cloves. Decorate with the mint sprigs and serve with a little plain yoghurt, crème fraîche or light sour cream.

mental energy *foods*

PROTEIN FOODS CONTAIN *amino acids that stimulate the brain and so encourage clear thinking. If you have a demanding day's work ahead of you, eat eggs or yoghurt and other dairy products for breakfast. Fish, chicken, lean meats and pulses are also excellent sources of protein. Note that protein foods eaten at night may overactivate the brain and keep you awake.*

Fish and shellfish contain an amino acid called tyrosine, used to make the brain-stimulating chemicals noradrenalin and dopamine, which increase mental energy and alertness.

warm chicken salad *with* mango

This appetising salad combines different textures and flavours. Cold-pressed oils and walnuts contain essential fatty acids needed by every cell in the body. They are especially important for healthy brain tissue and mental alertness.

ingredients

- 55g (2oz) baby spinach leaves
- 55g (2oz) watercress
- 175g (6oz) cherry tomatoes, halved
- 1 medium-sized ripe mango, peeled, stoned and diced
- 6–8 spring onions, chopped
- 55g (2oz) pitted black olives, roughly chopped
- 55g (2oz) walnuts, roughly chopped
- 1tbsp olive oil
- 225g (8oz) skinless, boneless chicken breast, cut into thin strips
- fresh herb sprigs, to garnish

for the dressing

- 2tbsp walnut oil
- 1tbsp olive oil
- 1tbsp red wine vinegar
- sea salt
- freshly ground black pepper

serves *four*
preparation time *15 minutes*
cooking time *5–7 minutes*

method

1 Put the spinach leaves, watercress, cherry tomatoes, mango, spring onions, olives and walnuts in a bowl and toss together. Divide the salad between four serving plates.

2 Put the walnut oil, olive oil, vinegar and seasoning in a small bowl and whisk until thoroughly mixed. Set aside.

3 Heat the remaining olive oil in a non-stick wok or large frying pan. Add the chicken and stir-fry over a medium heat for about 5–7 minutes, until cooked, tender and lightly browned all over.

4 Top each salad with some hot chicken, give the dressing a quick whisk, then drizzle a little dressing over each salad.

5 Garnish with the herb sprigs and serve with oatcakes, crispbread or wholemeal bread.

variations

- *Use skinless turkey breast or lean beef or lamb instead of chicken.*
- *Use 1 ripe avocado, peeled, stoned, diced and tossed in a little lemon juice, instead of the mango.*
- *Use pecan nuts or hazelnuts instead of walnuts.*
- *Use hazelnut oil or olive oil instead of walnut oil.*

creamy carrot *and* celeriac soup

This creamy soup is a delicious starter or snack. Carrots contain beta carotene, the plant form of vitamin A, which is an important antioxidant. Fresh culinary herbs such as coriander make this dish even more nutritious.

ingredients

- 25g (1oz) butter
- 1 large onion, chopped
- 350g (12oz) carrots, sliced
- 350g (12oz) celeriac, diced
- 600ml (1 pint) vegetable stock (see recipe on page 20)
- sea salt
- freshly ground black pepper
- 300ml (½ pint) milk
- 1–2tbsp chopped fresh coriander (optional)
- fresh coriander sprigs, to garnish

serves *four*
preparation time *15 minutes*
cooking time *40–45 minutes*

method

1 Melt the butter in a large saucepan. Add the onion, carrots and celeriac, and cook gently for 5 minutes, stirring occasionally.
2 Add the stock and seasoning, and stir. Cover, bring to the boil, then reduce the heat and simmer for 30–40 minutes, until the vegetables are cooked and tender, stirring occasionally.
3 Remove the pan from the heat and set aside to cool slightly, then purée the soup in a blender or food processor until smooth.
4 Return the soup to the rinsed-out saucepan, add the milk and chopped coriander, if using, and reheat gently until piping hot, stirring occasionally.
5 Ladle into warmed soup bowls to serve and garnish with the coriander sprigs.
6 Serve with warm wholemeal bread rolls.

variations

- *Use parsnips instead of celeriac.*
- *Use swede instead of carrots.*
- *Use chopped fresh mixed herbs or parsley instead of coriander.*

freezing instructions

Allow to cool completely, then transfer to a rigid, freezeproof container. Cover, seal and label. Freeze for up to 3 months. Defrost, and reheat gently in a saucepan until piping hot.

lemon sole *with* wild mushrooms

Grilled lemon sole fillets are delicious served with a wild mushroom sauce. Fish contains an amino acid used to make brain-stimulating chemicals that increase mental energy and alertness.

ingredients

- 25g (1oz) butter
- 2 shallots (French shallots), thinly sliced
- 1 clove garlic, crushed
- 350g (12oz) mixed fresh wild mushrooms, such as shiitake and oyster mushrooms, sliced
- 2tbsp dry sherry
- 2–3tsp chopped fresh thyme (optional)
- sea salt
- freshly ground black pepper
- 2tbsp crème fraîche or light sour cream
- 8 lemon sole fillets
- a little olive oil, for brushing
- fresh thyme sprigs, to garnish

serves *four*
preparation time *10 minutes*
cooking time *10–15 minutes*

method

1 Preheat the grill to medium. Line a grill rack with foil.

2 Melt the butter in a large non-stick frying pan. Add the shallots and garlic, and cook gently for 3 minutes, stirring occasionally.

3 Add the mushrooms and cook for about 5 minutes until tender, stirring occasionally.

4 Stir in the sherry, chopped thyme, if using, and seasoning. Increase the heat slightly and cook for 2–3 minutes, stirring until most of the liquid has evaporated.

5 Stir in the crème fraîche and adjust the seasoning.

6 Meanwhile, cook the fish. Place the lemon sole fillets on the grill rack and brush them lightly all over with oil. Grill for 4–6 minutes, until the fish is cooked and the flesh just flakes when tested with a fork, carefully turning over once during cooking.

7 Place two fillets on each warmed serving plate and spoon some mushroom sauce on top or alongside. Garnish with the thyme sprigs and serve with sautéed potatoes, cooked green cabbage and baby sweetcorn.

variations

- *Use firm white fish steaks instead of lemon sole (increase the cooking time a little).*
- *Use button mushrooms instead of wild ones.*
- *Use brandy instead of sherry.*
- *Use chopped fresh sage or tarragon instead of thyme.*

prawn pasta salad

In this tasty dish, cooked pasta, vegetables, prawns and avocado are tossed together in a mayonnaise dressing. Prawns contain the mineral zinc, which is necessary for a healthy brain and nervous system.

ingredients

- 225g (8oz) pasta twists (spirals)
- 225g (8oz) small broccoli florets
- 55g (2oz) round (butterhead) lettuce, shredded
- 55g (2oz) watercress, chopped
- 225g (8oz) cooked, peeled prawns
- 1 ripe avocado
- 1tbsp fresh lemon juice
- fresh chives, to garnish

for the dressing

- 8tbsp mayonnaise (see recipe on page 21)
- 2tbsp chopped fresh chives
- 1tsp finely grated lemon rind
- sea salt
- freshly ground black pepper

serves *four to six*
preparation time *10 minutes*
cooking time *10 minutes*

method

1 Cook the pasta until just cooked or *al dente*. Drain, rinse under cold running water, and drain thoroughly again. Set aside to cool completely.

2 Blanch the broccoli in a saucepan of boiling water for 3 minutes. Cool under cold running water, then drain thoroughly and set aside.

3 Put the cold pasta in a large bowl. In a small bowl, mix the mayonnaise, chopped chives, lemon rind and seasoning. Add to the pasta and mix well.

4 Stir in the broccoli, lettuce, watercress and prawns. Peel, stone and dice the avocado and toss with the lemon juice. Add to the pasta salad and stir gently.

5 Serve immediately, or cover and chill before serving.

6 Garnish with the chives and serve with crusty wholemeal bread rolls.

variations

- *Use chopped fresh basil or parsley instead of chives.*
- *Use finely grated lime or orange rind instead of lemon rind.*
- *Use canned flaked tuna or salmon instead of prawns.*

kidney kebabs *with* herbed rice

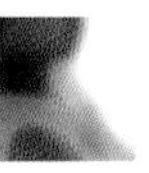

Succulent lamb's kidneys with mixed vegetables make tasty kebabs. Lamb's kidneys provide B vitamins, which are essential for healthy brain function.

ingredients

- 225g (8oz) long grain brown rice
- 12 small shallots (French shallots)
- 12 baby sweetcorn
- 350g (12oz) lamb's kidneys, cored and quartered
- 2 small red peppers (capsicums), each cut into 8 pieces
- 1 courgette (zucchini), cut into 16 thin slices
- 8 bay leaves
- 6tbsp red wine
- 2tbsp olive oil
- 2tsp English mustard
- 1 clove garlic, crushed
- sea salt
- freshly ground black pepper
- 2–3tbsp chopped fresh mixed herbs

serves ***four***
preparation time ***15 minutes***
cooking time ***35 minutes***

method

1 Cook the rice until tender, drain and keep it warm.

2 Meanwhile, cook the shallots and sweetcorn in boiling water for 5 minutes. Drain, rinse under cold water to cool, then drain again.

3 Preheat the grill to medium. Thread the kidneys, red peppers, courgette, shallots, sweetcorn and bay leaves onto four long skewers, dividing the ingredients equally between them.

4 Put the red wine, oil, mustard, garlic and seasoning in a small bowl and whisk.

5 Arrange the kebabs on a rack in a grill pan and brush generously all over with the mustard mixture.

6 Grill for 10–15 minutes, turning occasionally, until the kidneys and vegetables are cooked and tender. Brush the kebabs frequently with the mustard mixture to prevent them drying out.

7 Stir the chopped herbs and seasoning into the hot rice, then spoon the herbed rice onto a warmed serving dish. Place the kebabs on top and serve with a mixed dark-green leaf salad.

Variations

- *Use a mixture of wild rice and brown rice.*
- *Use cubed lean lamb instead of some or all of the kidneys.*
- *Use unsweetened apple juice instead of red wine.*
- *Use button mushrooms instead of baby sweetcorn.*
- *Use baby (pickling) onions instead of shallots.*

braised chicken *with* celery *and* mushrooms

Tender chicken breasts braised with celery and mushrooms, served with mashed potatoes or rice and cooked fresh vegetables, makes a nutritious main meal. Chicken is a high-protein food, important for good brain function.

ingredients

- 1tbsp olive oil
- 4 skinless, boneless chicken breasts
- 1 onion, sliced
- 6 sticks celery, sliced
- 2 parsnips, cut into large cubes
- 225g (8oz) mushrooms, sliced
- 225g (8oz) baby button mushrooms
- 55g (2oz) whole green lentils
- 300ml (½ pint) chicken stock (see recipe on page 20)
- 200ml (7fl oz) dry or medium-dry white wine
- sea salt
- freshly ground black pepper
- 1tbsp cornflour (optional)
- 15ml (1tbsp) chopped fresh tarragon (optional)
- fresh herb sprigs, to garnish

serves ***four***
preparation time ***15 minutes***
cooking time ***1 hour***

method

1 Preheat the oven to 180°C/350°F/gas mark 4.

2 Heat the oil in a large flameproof, ovenproof casserole dish. Add the chicken and cook until sealed all over, turning occasionally. Remove the chicken from the dish and set aside.

3 Add the onion and celery to the casserole dish and cook gently for 5 minutes, stirring occasionally.

4 Return the chicken to the dish and add all the remaining ingredients, except the cornflour, chopped tarragon and herb garnish. Stir, then bring to the boil, stirring occasionally.

5 Cover and bake for about 1 hour, until the chicken, vegetables and lentils are cooked and tender, stirring once or twice.

6 To thicken the sauce slightly, remove the chicken from the casserole with a slotted spoon. Place on a warmed plate, cover and keep hot. Blend the cornflour with 2tbsp water and stir into the casserole.

7 Bring slowly to the boil, stirring continuously, until the sauce thickens slightly, then simmer gently for 2 minutes, stirring. Stir in the chopped tarragon, if using.

8 Serve the chicken with the vegetable sauce spooned over.

9 Garnish with the herb sprigs and serve with fresh vegetables, such as mashed potatoes and broccoli florets.

variations

- *Use small turkey breast steaks instead of chicken.*
- *Use 2 carrots instead of parsnips.*
- *Use 2 leeks instead of the onion.*
- *Use brown lentils instead of green.*

freezing instructions

Allow to cool completely, then transfer to a rigid, freezeproof container. Cover, seal and label. Freeze for up to 3 months. Defrost completely, and reheat in a moderate oven until piping hot.

crunchy coleslaw *with* mustard dressing

Fresh raw vegetables, nuts and dried fruits are tossed in a delicious mustard dressing to make this crunchy coleslaw. Nuts contain boron, a deficiency of which can impair mental alertness.

ingredients

- 225g (8oz) green cabbage
- 225g (8oz) carrots
- 175g (6oz) small cauliflower florets
- 115g (4oz) sultanas
- 85g (3oz) raisins
- 55g (2oz) ready-to-eat dried peaches, chopped
- 85g (3oz) mixed nuts, such as almonds, cashews and pecans, chopped
- fresh watercress sprigs, to garnish

for the dressing

- 6tbsp mayonnaise (see recipe on page 21)
- 6tbsp plain yoghurt
- 1tbsp wholegrain mustard
- sea salt
- freshly ground black pepper

serves *six*
preparation time *15 minutes, plus 1 hour chilling time*

method

1 Shred the cabbage, coarsely grate the carrots, and put them in a large serving bowl.
2 Halve the cauliflower florets and stir into the bowl with the mixed dried fruit and nuts.
3 Put the mayonnaise, yoghurt, mustard and seasoning in a small bowl and mix well.
4 Add the mayonnaise dressing to the cabbage mixture and mix well. Cover and refrigerate for at least 1 hour before serving.
5 Garnish with the watercress sprigs and serve with oven-baked potatoes topped with a little Cheddar or goat's cheese.

variations

- *Use white or red cabbage instead of green cabbage.*
- *Use ready-to-eat dried apricots or pears instead of peaches.*
- *Add more dressing to taste.*

curried sweet potato *and* leek purée

This tasty purée of sweet potatoes and leeks, flavoured with ground spices, is a tasty alternative to mashed potatoes. Sweet potatoes are a good source of beta carotene (for vitamin A) and vitamin C, both good brain foods.

ingredients

- 700g (1lb 9oz) sweet potatoes, diced
- 225g (8oz) leeks, washed and finely chopped
- 1tsp ground cumin
- 1tsp ground coriander
- 1tsp ground turmeric
- 1 clove garlic, crushed
- 55g (2oz) Cheddar cheese, finely grated
- 2tbsp hot milk
- 1tbsp chopped fresh coriander
- sea salt
- freshly ground black pepper
- fresh coriander sprigs, to garnish

serves ***four***
preparation time *10 minutes*
cooking time *10–15 minutes*

method

1 Cook the potatoes in a saucepan of boiling water for 10–15 minutes, until cooked and tender. Drain thoroughly, then mash well until very smooth. Cover and keep hot.

2 Meanwhile, steam the leeks over a saucepan of boiling water for 10–15 minutes, until tender. Drain well, pressing out any excess water with the back of a spoon.

3 Add the leeks to the mashed potatoes with the ground spices, garlic, cheese, milk, coriander and seasoning, and mix well.

4 Garnish with the coriander sprigs and serve with oven-roasted mixed vegetables or grilled lean meat or fish.

variations

- *The ground spices can be omitted, or add 1–2tsp curry powder instead.*
- *Use standard potatoes instead of sweet potatoes.*
- *Use chopped fresh parsley or basil instead of coriander.*

vegetable ragout *with* wholemeal crust

Serve this pastry-topped vegetable ragout with new potatoes and green vegetables. Vegetables are a good source of vitamin C, which aids the absorption of iron – an essential nutrient for clear thinking.

ingredients

- 1 onion, sliced
- 1 clove garlic, crushed
- 1 carrot, thinly sliced
- 1 courgette (zucchini), sliced
- 2 sticks celery, chopped
- 1 small green pepper (capsicum), seeded and diced
- 115g (4oz) mushrooms, sliced
- 400g (14oz) can tomatoes, chopped
- 4tbsp medium cider
- 2tsp dried mixed herbs
- 115g (4oz) frozen peas
- a little beaten egg, to glaze
- fresh herb sprigs, to garnish

for the pastry

- 115g (4oz) plain wholemeal flour
- sea salt and black pepper
- 55g (2oz) butter, chopped
- 25g (1oz) fresh Parmesan cheese, finely grated
- 1tbsp chopped fresh chives
- 1tbsp chopped fresh parsley

serves *four*
preparation time *40 minutes*
cooking time *25–30 minutes*

method

1 To make the pastry, put the flour and a pinch of salt in a bowl, then rub in the butter until the mixture resembles breadcrumbs.
2 Stir in the Parmesan cheese and herbs, then add enough cold water to form a soft dough. Wrap and chill for 30 minutes.
3 Meanwhile, place all the remaining ingredients, except the peas, beaten egg and herb garnish, in a large saucepan of water and stir. Cover, bring to the boil, then reduce the heat and simmer for 15 minutes, stirring occasionally. Uncover, increase the heat slightly and cook for a further 10 minutes, stirring occasionally.
4 Stir in the peas and season to taste with salt and pepper. Spoon the vegetables into an ovenproof pie dish.
5 Preheat the oven to 200°C/400°F/gas mark 6.
6 Roll the pastry out on a lightly floured surface to a shape a little larger than the pie dish.
7 Place the pastry over the vegetable mixture in the pie dish, trim off excess and reserve the trimmings. Scallop or decorate the pastry edges and make a hole in the centre of the pastry lid. Garnish the pie with pastry trimmings and brush with a little beaten egg to glaze.
8 Bake for 25–30 minutes, until the pastry is crisp and lightly browned.
9 Garnish with the herb sprigs and serve hot with fresh vegetables, such as new potatoes and chopped spinach leaves or green beans.

variations

- *Use Cheddar cheese instead of Parmesan cheese.*
- *Use frozen broad beans instead of peas.*
- *Use 1 red or yellow pepper instead of the green pepper.*
- *Use white wine or vegetable stock instead of cider.*

triple berry cobbler

This delicious fruit dessert, served with home-made custard, plain yoghurt, crème fraîche or light sour cream, makes a popular family treat. Berries provide vitamin C, which is important for healthy brain function.

ingredients

- 700g (1lb 9oz) mixed ripe raspberries, blackberries and blueberries
- 2tbsp unsweetened apple juice
- 55g (2oz) light brown sugar

for the scones

- 175g (6oz) plain wholemeal flour
- 55g (2oz) fine oatmeal
- 2tsp baking powder
- 1tsp ground mixed spice
- 55g (2oz) butter, chopped
- 55g (2oz) light brown sugar
- 1 banana, peeled and mashed with a little lemon juice
- about 4tbsp milk, plus extra for glazing

serves *four to six*
preparation time *20 minutes*
cooking time *15–20 minutes*

method

1 Preheat the oven to 220°C/425°F/gas mark 7.

2 Put the berries and apple juice in a saucepan. Cover and cook gently for about 10 minutes, until softened. Remove the pan from the heat and stir in the sugar. Transfer the berry mixture to an ovenproof dish.

3 Meanwhile, mix the flour, oatmeal, baking powder and mixed spice in a bowl, then lightly rub in the butter until the mixture resembles breadcrumbs.

4 Stir in the sugar, then stir in the mashed banana and enough milk to make a soft dough.

5 Turn the dough out onto a lightly floured surface and knead gently. Roll or pat out the dough and cut into 8 or 10 rounds, using a 5cm (2in) fluted cutter.

6 Arrange the scones round the edge of the ovenproof dish on top of the fruit, overlapping them slightly. Brush the scones with a little milk to glaze.

7 Bake for 15–20 minutes, until the scones are risen and golden brown.

8 Serve with home-made custard, plain yoghurt, crème fraîche or light sour cream.

variations

- *Cut the scone dough into squares or triangles instead of rounds.*
- *Use another fruit mixture, such as apples, pears and peaches, instead of berries.*
- *Use ground cinnamon or ginger instead of mixed spice.*

apple *and* apricot scone round

This fruity scone round is delicious spread with butter, honey or preserve. Dried apricots contain minerals essential to a healthy brain.

ingredients

- 225g (8oz) plain wholemeal flour
- pinch of salt
- 2tsp baking powder
- 1tsp ground cinnamon
- 55g (2oz) butter, chopped
- 25g (1oz) light brown sugar
- 85g (3oz) ready-to-eat dried apricots, finely chopped
- 1 medium cooking apple, about 310g (11oz) in weight, peeled, cored and coarsely grated
- about 3–4tbsp milk, plus extra for glazing
- 1tbsp sugar

serves *eight*
preparation time *15 minutes*
cooking time *25–30 minutes*

method

1 Preheat the oven to 200°C/400°F/gas mark 6.
2 Line a baking tray with non-stick baking paper.
3 Put the flour, salt, baking powder and cinnamon in a bowl. Lightly rub in the chopped butter until the mixture resembles breadcrumbs.
4 Stir in the sugar, apricots and apple, and enough milk to make a soft dough.
5 Turn the dough out onto a lightly floured surface, knead gently and shape into an 18cm (7in) round. Place on the baking tray, brush with milk and sprinkle with sugar. Mark into eight wedges.
6 Bake for 25–30 minutes, until risen and golden brown. Transfer to a wire rack to cool and break into wedges to serve.
7 Serve warm or cold spread with butter, honey or preserve.

variations

- *Use sultanas or chopped ready-to-eat dried pineapple, pears or peaches instead of apricots.*
- *Use ground mixed spice instead of cinnamon.*

blueberry brûlée

These delicious blueberry brûlées are truly irresistible. Blueberries are a good source of vitamin C, which helps the absorption of iron.

ingredients

- 350g (12oz) blueberries
- 1tbsp unsweetened apple juice
- 1tbsp honey
- 200g (7oz) plain yoghurt
- 200g (7oz) crème fraîche or light sour cream
- 55g (2oz) sugar
- fresh mint sprigs, to decorate

serves *four to six*
preparation time *10 minutes, plus 3 hours' chilling time*
cooking time *15 minutes*

method

1 Put the blueberries in a saucepan with the apple juice and honey. Cover and cook gently for about 10 minutes, until the fruit is just softened. Remove the pan from the heat, uncover and set aside to cool completely.
2 When cold, spoon the blueberries into ramekins.
3 Fold the yoghurt and crème fraîche or light sour cream together and spread evenly over the top of the blueberries, to cover completely. Chill for 3 hours.
4 Preheat the grill to high. Sprinkle the sugar evenly over the yoghurt mixture and place the dishes under the grill for a few minutes, until the sugar melts and caramelises. Cool and chill.
5 Decorate with the mint sprigs, and serve with fresh fruit, such as raspberries and peaches.

variations

- *Use blackberries or raspberries instead of blueberries.*
- *Use maple syrup instead of honey.*
- *Add 1tsp finely grated lemon or orange rind to the cooked fruit.*

an interested party

THESE INSPIRING RECIPES *from the mental energy foods section contain all the nutrients you need to encourage clear thinking, such as protein, B vitamins, vitamin C and the amino acid tyrosine which activates brain-stimulating chemicals. So eat up when you've got a tough assignment ahead.*

creamy carrot *and* celeriac soup

Kick off your meal with carrots for beta carotene – a vital nutrient for mental agility.

ingredients

- 25g (1oz) butter
- 1 large onion, chopped
- 350g (12oz) carrots, sliced
- 350g (12oz) celeriac, diced
- 600ml (1 pint) vegetable stock (see recipe on page 20)
- sea salt
- freshly ground black pepper
- 300ml (½ pint) milk
- 1–2tbsp chopped fresh coriander (optional)
- fresh coriander sprigs, to garnish

serves *four*
preparation time *15 minutes*
cooking time *40–45 minutes*

method

1 Melt the butter in a large saucepan. Add the onion, carrots and celeriac, and cook gently for 5 minutes, stirring occasionally.
2 Add the stock and seasoning, and stir. Cover, bring to the boil, then reduce the heat and simmer for 30–40 minutes, until the vegetables are cooked and tender.
3 Remove the pan from the heat and set aside to cool slightly, then purée the soup in a blender or food processor until smooth.
4 Return the soup to the rinsed-out saucepan, add the milk and chopped coriander, if using, and reheat gently until piping hot, stirring occasionally.
5 Ladle into warmed soup bowls.

vegetable ragout *with* wholemeal crust

The vegetables in this ragout provide vitamin C to help absorb the iron necessary to focus your thinking.

ingredients

- 1 onion, sliced
- 1 clove garlic, crushed
- 1 carrot, thinly sliced
- 1 courgette (zucchini), sliced
- 2 sticks celery, chopped
- 1 small green pepper (capsicum), seeded and diced
- 115g (4oz) mushrooms, sliced
- 400g (14oz) can tomatoes, chopped
- 4tbsp medium cider
- 2tsp dried mixed herbs

- 115g (4oz) frozen peas
- a little beaten egg, to glaze
- fresh herb sprigs, to garnish

for the pastry

- 115g (4oz) plain wholemeal flour
- sea salt and black pepper
- 55g (2oz) butter, chopped
- 25g (1oz) fresh Parmesan cheese, finely grated
- 1tbsp chopped fresh chives
- 1tbsp chopped fresh parsley

serves *four*
preparation time *40 minutes*
cooking time *25–30 minutes*

method

1 To make the pastry, put the flour and a pinch of salt in a bowl, then rub in the butter until the mixture resembles breadcrumbs.

2 Stir in the Parmesan cheese and herbs, then add enough cold water to form a soft dough. Wrap and chill for 30 minutes.

3 Meanwhile, place all the remaining ingredients, except the peas, beaten egg and herb garnish, in a large saucepan of water and stir. Cover, bring to the boil, then reduce the heat and simmer for 15 minutes, stirring occasionally. Uncover, increase the heat slightly and cook for a further 10 minutes, stirring occasionally.

4 Stir in the peas and season to taste with salt and pepper. Spoon the vegetables into an ovenproof pie dish.

5 Preheat the oven to 200°C/400°F/gas mark 6.

6 Roll the pastry out on a lightly floured surface to a shape a little larger than the pie dish.

7 Place the pastry over the vegetable mixture in the pie dish, trim off excess and reserve the trimmings. Scallop or decorate the pastry edges and make a hole in the centre of the pastry lid. Garnish the pie with pastry trimmings and brush with a little beaten egg to glaze.

8 Bake for 25–30 minutes, until the pastry is crisp and lightly browned.

9 Garnish with the herb sprigs and serve hot with fresh vegetables, such as new potatoes and chopped spinach leaves or green beans.

blueberry brûlée

Blueberries are high in vitamin C, which aids iron absorption.

ingredients

- 350g (12oz) blueberries
- 1tbsp unsweetened apple juice
- 1tbsp honey
- 200g (7oz) plain yoghurt
- 200g (7oz) crème fraîche or light sour cream
- 55g (2oz) cane sugar
- fresh mint sprigs, to decorate

serves *four to six*
preparation time *10 minutes, plus 3 hours' chilling time*
cooking time *15 minutes*

method

1 Put the blueberries in a saucepan with the apple juice and honey. Cover and cook gently for about 10 minutes, until the fruit is just softened. Remove the pan from the heat, uncover and set aside to cool completely.

2 When cold, spoon the blueberries into ramekins.

3 Fold the yoghurt and crème fraîche or light sour cream together and spread evenly over the top of the blueberries, to cover completely. Chill for 3 hours.

4 Preheat the grill to high. Sprinkle the sugar evenly over the yoghurt mixture and place the dishes under the grill for a few minutes, until the sugar melts and caramelises. Cool and chill.

5 Decorate with the mint sprigs, and serve with fresh fruit, such as raspberries and peaches.

mood

In this Mood section we suggest nutritious recipes to balance your blood sugar levels, which will help to reduce mood swings and feelings of lethargy. We encourage you to experiment and discover which foods suit your unique moods; whether you want to feel wide awake, inspired or calm.

B group vitamins are required to support normal brain functions. Vitamin B_3 (niacin), B_5 (pantothenic acid), B_6 and B_{12}, plus iron – another brilliant brain energiser – are all found in meats, poultry, eggs, fish, wholegrains and enriched cereals. Many of these foods also contain the amino acid tryptophan, which is known to relax the brain, reduce feelings of stress and encourage deeper sleep. Magnesium and calcium are sometimes known as nature's tranquilisers, so if you want to remain calm

FOODS

and sleep well, try eating almonds, cashew nuts, cheese, yoghurt, leafy green vegetables, pulses and tofu, and before bed drink a glass of warm milk.

Vitamin C not only supports immune function within the body, it is also vital when the brain is tired or under stress. Mood swings, including some types of depression, may be signs of a deficiency of vitamins B and C. Citrus fruit, peppers (capsicums), parsley, broccoli, lemons and watercress are good sources of vitamin C. Seeds, nuts and oily fish are rich in the essential fatty acids which are needed to make every cell and hormone within the body. Treats such as chocolate help to elevate mood as they contain phenylalanine, an amino acid that helps you to feel good. But remember the magic words – balance in all things, including your diet. Enjoy!

relaxing *foods*

IF YOU FEEL *like a coiled spring at the end of the working day and need to wind down, then a dish featuring complex carbohydrates, such as brown rice, pasta, noodles, couscous or potato, makes an ideal evening meal. A small bowl of muesli or any oat-based cereal, or a mashed banana with yoghurt, about an hour before bedtime, can encourage sounder sleep. By eating complex carbohydrates you can increase levels of serotonin, the brain chemical that is known for its calming and soothing properties. Feelings of serenity, security and tranquillity are all associated with adequate levels of serotonin.*

green salad *with* avocado dressing

Serve this refreshing salad with wholemeal bread as a starter or snack. Dark green salad leaves are rich in many nutrients, including iron, B vitamins, vitamin C, calcium and magnesium, all of which are needed for brain function.

ingredients

- 140g (5oz) mixed dark-green salad leaves, such as baby spinach, lollo rosso (coral lettuce), red (ruby) chard and rocket
- 55g (2oz) watercress
- 1 green pepper (capsicum), seeded and sliced
- half a cucumber, thinly sliced
- 6–8 spring onions, chopped
- 55–85g (2–3oz) walnuts, roughly chopped

for the dressing

- 1 large avocado
- finely grated rind and juice of 1 lemon
- 6tbsp plain yoghurt
- 1tsp Dijon mustard
- sea salt
- freshly ground black pepper

serves *four to six*
preparation time *15 minutes*

method

1 Put the salad leaves in a large bowl. Add the watercress, green pepper, cucumber and spring onions, and toss together. Divide the salad among four or six serving plates or bowls.
2 To make the dressing, peel, stone and chop the avocado, and place in a food processor with the lemon rind and juice. Purée until smooth. Add the yoghurt, mustard and seasoning, and blend.
3 Spoon some dressing over each salad, sprinkle with the walnuts and serve with crusty wholemeal bread.

variation

- *Use the finely grated rind and juice of 1 lime instead of the lemon.*

summer lettuce soup

This refreshing summer soup makes an ideal starter or light lunch. Lettuce contains beta carotene, potassium, vitamin C and some calcium. It is often used by herbalists as a calming food.

ingredients

- 1tbsp olive oil
- 1 onion, chopped
- 225g (8oz) potatoes, diced
- 225g (8oz) round (butterhead) lettuce, shredded
- 300ml (½ pint) chicken stock (see recipe on page 20)
- 300ml (½ pint) milk
- sea salt
- freshly ground black pepper
- 2tbsp chopped fresh parsley
- 2tbsp single (pouring) cream, to garnish (optional)

serves *four*
preparation time *10 minutes*
cooking time *25–30 minutes*

method

1 Heat the oil in a large saucepan. Add the onion and potatoes and cook gently for about 5 minutes, stirring occasionally, until soft.
2 Add the lettuce and cook gently for 2 minutes, then add the stock, milk and seasoning, and stir.
3 Cover, bring to the boil, then reduce the heat and simmer for 15 minutes until the vegetables are tender, stirring occasionally,.
4 Remove the pan from the heat and allow to cool slightly, then purée the soup in a blender or food processor until smooth.
5 Return the soup to the rinsed-out saucepan, stir in the chopped parsley, then reheat gently until piping hot, stirring occasionally.
6 Ladle into warmed soup bowls to serve and garnish each serving with a swirl of cream, if liked.
7 Serve with wholemeal rolls.

variations

- *Use spinach instead of lettuce.*
- *Use sweet potatoes instead of standard potatoes.*
- *Use 1 leek instead of the onion.*

freezing instructions

Allow to cool completely, then transfer to a rigid, freezeproof container. Cover, seal and label. Freeze for up to 3 months. Defrost, and reheat gently in a saucepan until piping hot.

poached eggs *with* tuna mayonnaise

Poached eggs served with tuna mayonnaise makes an appetising snack or starter. Tuna provides iron and magnesium, which are vital for a healthy nervous system. Yoghurt, like other forms of milk, contains tryptophan, which the brain converts into the soothing chemical serotonin.

ingredients

- 185g (6½oz) can tuna in water, drained and mashed
- 4tbsp mayonnaise (see recipe on page 21)
- 2tbsp plain yoghurt
- 2 spring onions, finely chopped
- 1tsp finely grated lemon rind
- sea salt
- freshly ground black pepper
- 4 medium eggs
- shredded round (butterhead) lettuce leaves and watercress, to garnish

serves *four*
preparation time *10 minutes*
cooking time *4–6 minutes*

method

1 Put the tuna, mayonnaise, yoghurt, spring onions, lemon rind and seasoning in a bowl and mix thoroughly. Cover and chill while poaching the eggs.

2 Fill a frying pan or saucepan with water to a depth of about 7.5cm (3in). Bring to the boil, then swirl the water with a spoon. Crack the eggs and slip them into the water, one by one. Cook gently for a few minutes until lightly set, or longer if you prefer firmer eggs.

3 Carefully remove the eggs from the pan using a slotted spoon and place each one on a serving plate. Spoon some tuna mayonnaise alongside and garnish each serving with a little lettuce and watercress.

4 Serve with oatcakes, crispbread or wholemeal toast.

variations

- *Boil the eggs instead of poaching.*
- *Spread the tuna mayonnaise over wholemeal toast and top with a poached egg.*
- *Add 1 small clove garlic, crushed, to the tuna mayonnaise.*
- *Use canned red or pink salmon instead of tuna.*

salmon, pepper *and* mushroom wholemeal pizza

Pizzas are always a popular family meal, and the addition of salmon provides extra B vitamins, which help to maintain a healthy nervous system. Fresh vegetables are rich in vitamin C, so you can replenish your stocks with the pepper and tomato on this delicious pizza.

ingredients

- 1tbsp olive oil
- 4 shallots (French shallots), sliced
- 1 red pepper (capsicum), seeded and sliced
- 225g (8oz) mushrooms, sliced
- 1 clove garlic, crushed
- 4tbsp passata (sieved tomatoes)
- 4 sun-dried tomatoes in oil, drained and finely chopped
- 1–2tbsp chopped fresh mixed herbs
- sea salt
- freshly ground black pepper
- 213g (7½oz) can salmon in water, drained and flaked
- 2 plum (Roma) tomatoes, sliced
- 115g (4oz) Cheddar cheese, grated
- fresh herb sprigs, to garnish

for the pizza base

- 175g (6oz) plain wholemeal flour
- 55g (2oz) fine oatmeal
- pinch of salt
- 2tsp baking powder
- 55g (2oz) butter, chopped
- about 100ml (3½fl oz) milk

serves *four to six*
preparation time *25 minutes*
cooking time *25–30 minutes*

method

1 Preheat the oven to 220°C/425°F/gas mark 7.
2 Line a baking tray with non-stick baking paper.
3 Heat the oil in a saucepan, add the shallots, pepper, mushrooms and garlic. Cook gently for 10 minutes, stirring occasionally, until soft.
4 Meanwhile, make the pizza base. Put the flour, oatmeal, salt and baking powder in a bowl and lightly rub in the butter until the mixture resembles breadcrumbs. Add enough milk to form a soft but not sticky dough.
5 Roll the dough out on a lightly floured surface to a circle roughly 25cm (10in) in diameter. Place the dough on the baking tray and make the edges slightly thicker than the centre.
6 Mix the passata, sun-dried tomatoes, chopped herbs and seasoning together and spread over the pizza base.
7 Spoon the cooked vegetables over the base, scatter over the salmon and top with the tomato slices. Sprinkle the cheese evenly over the top.
8 Bake for 25–30 minutes, until cooked and golden brown.
9 Garnish with the herb sprigs and serve hot or cold with crusty wholemeal bread and a pepper and tomato salad.

variations

- *Use canned tuna instead of salmon.*
- *Use courgettes (zucchini) or aubergines (eggplants) instead of mushrooms.*

freezing instructions

Allow to cool completely, then wrap in foil, seal and label. Freeze for up to 3 months. Defrost, and reheat in a moderate oven until piping hot.

pilchards *in* herbed oatmeal

Oily fish such as pilchards tossed in a herbed oatmeal mixture and lightly grilled makes a light evening meal or lunchtime dish. Enriched oatmeal is a good source of B vitamins and iron, which are important nutrients for the brain and for a healthy nervous system.

ingredients

- 115g (4oz) medium oatmeal
- 2tbsp chopped fresh mixed herbs
- finely grated rind of 1 lemon
- sea salt
- freshly ground black pepper
- 8 pilchard fillets
- 1 medium egg, beaten
- lemon wedges and fresh parsley sprigs, to garnish

serves *four*
preparation time *10 minutes*
cooking time *6–8 minutes*

method

1 Cover a grill rack with foil and preheat the grill to high.
2 Put the oatmeal, chopped herbs, lemon rind and seasoning in a bowl and mix well.
3 Brush each fish fillet all over with a little beaten egg and place on a plate. Coat each fillet with the oatmeal mixture, shaking off any excess.
4 Place the fish on the grill rack and grill for 6–8 minutes, turning once, until the fish is cooked and the flesh just flakes when tested with a fork.
5 Garnish with lemon wedges and the parsley sprigs and serve with lightly buttered wholemeal bread.

variations

- *Use any other oily fish fillets.*
- *Use chopped fresh parsley or chives instead of mixed herbs.*
- *Use the finely grated rind of 1 lime or 1 small orange instead of the lemon rind.*

lamb's kidney *and* mixed bean risotto

This flavoursome risotto is delicious topped with a little grated Cheddar or fresh Parmesan cheese. Kidneys are a good source of B vitamins, which are essential for healthy brain function. The complex carbohydrates found in brown rice may increase levels of serotonin, a brain chemical known for its calming properties.

ingredients

- 400ml (14fl oz) hot vegetable stock (see recipe on page 20)
- 1tbsp olive oil
- 1 onion, chopped
- 1 clove garlic, crushed
- 1 green pepper (capsicum), seeded and diced
- 2 sticks celery, chopped
- 175g (6oz) mushrooms, sliced
- 350g (12oz) lamb's kidneys, cored and diced
- 400g (14oz) can black-eye beans, rinsed and drained
- 400g (14oz) can red kidney beans, rinsed and drained
- 225g (8oz) brown rice
- 350ml (12fl oz) dry white wine
- 2tbsp chopped fresh flatleaf parsley
- sea salt
- freshly ground black pepper
- fresh flatleaf parsley sprigs, to garnish

serves *four to six*
preparation time *10 minutes*
cooking time *40–45 minutes*

method

1 Bring the vegetable stock to the boil and keep hot.

2 Heat the oil in a separate large saucepan. Add the onion, garlic, green pepper and celery, and cook for 5 minutes, stirring occasionally, until soft.

3 Add the mushrooms, kidneys, mixed beans, rice, wine and a little stock, and stir. Bring to the boil, reduce the heat and simmer, uncovered, until almost all the liquid has been absorbed.

4 Continue adding the hot stock, a ladleful at a time, until the rice is cooked and creamy but still *al dente*, stirring occasionally. Add a little extra stock or wine, if necessary.

5 Stir the chopped parsley into the risotto, then season to taste with salt and pepper.

6 Garnish with the parsley sprigs and serve hot with a mixed dark-green leaf salad.

variations

- *Use courgettes (zucchini) instead of mushrooms.*
- *Use canned chickpeas instead of black-eye beans.*
- *Use 6 shallots (French shallots) or 1 leek instead of the onion.*

freezing instructions

Allow to cool completely, then transfer to a rigid, freezeproof container. Cover, seal and label. Freeze for up to 3 months. Defrost completely, and reheat gently in a saucepan until piping hot, adding a little extra stock, if necessary.

barbecued chicken *with* shallots

This chicken dish, served with a hot and spicy relish, can be cooked on a barbecue or in the oven. Chicken is a good source of protein and B vitamins, which are essential for healthy brain function.

ingredients

- 3tbsp olive oil
- 1tbsp cajun seasoning
- 6 skinless chicken legs or breast portions
- 450g (1lb) shallots (French shallots), halved
- fresh herb sprigs, to garnish

for the relish

- 400g (14oz) can tomatoes, chopped
- 1 onion, finely chopped
- 1 small fresh red chilli, seeded and finely chopped
- 1 clove garlic, crushed
- 1tbsp light brown sugar
- 1tbsp Worcestershire sauce
- 1tbsp red wine vinegar
- 1tbsp tomato purée (paste)
- ½tsp English mustard
- sea salt
- freshly ground black pepper

serves *six*
preparation time *10 minutes*
cooking time *45 minutes*

method

1 Preheat the oven to 200°C/400°F/gas mark 6.
2 Mix the oil and cajun seasoning in a bowl. Place the chicken portions and shallots in a roasting tin and brush all over with the oil.
3 Bake for about 45 minutes, until the chicken is cooked through and tender.
4 Meanwhile, put all the relish ingredients in a saucepan and stir. Bring to the boil, then simmer, uncovered, for 15–20 minutes, until the sauce is cooked and thickened, stirring occasionally.
5 Put the chicken and shallots onto warmed serving plates, spoon some relish alongside and garnish with the herb sprigs.
6 Serve with cooked fresh vegetables, such as baby (Dutch) carrots and courgettes (zucchini) and oven-baked potatoes.

variations

- *Cook the chicken on a barbecue instead of in the oven.*
- *Use ½–1tsp hot chilli powder instead of the fresh chilli.*

root vegetable rösti

The Swiss word rösti means 'crisp and golden'. Try this rösti of root vegetables for an appetising side dish or light meal. High-carbohydrate root vegetables can help boost serotonin, the stress-busting, tranquilising hormone. Fresh chives contain vitamin C and a little iron.

ingredients

- 225g (8oz) medium-sized potatoes
- 2 medium carrots
- 2 small parsnips
- 2tbsp chopped fresh chives
- sea salt
- freshly ground black pepper
- 2tbsp olive oil
- 1 small onion, finely chopped
- fresh chives, to garnish

serves *four*
preparation time *15 minutes*
cooking time *15–20 minutes*

method

1 Peel the potatoes, carrots and parsnips and cook them in a saucepan of lightly salted, boiling water for 6 minutes. Drain well and set aside to cool.
2 When cool enough to handle, grate the parboiled vegetables into a bowl and stir in the chopped chives and seasoning.
3 Heat the oil in a 25cm (10in) non-stick frying pan, add the onion and cook for about 5 minutes, until softened, stirring occasionally.
4 Add the vegetable mixture, stir, then form into a cake the size of the frying pan, pressing down gently. Fry over a medium heat until golden brown underneath.
5 Carefully turn the cake over, using a wide spatula, or turn it out onto a plate and slide it back into the pan. Cook until the other side is browned and crisp.
6 Cut into wedges and garnish with the chives.
7 Serve with cooked fresh vegetables, such as green beans and baby spinach leaves.

variations

- *Use sweet potatoes instead of standard potatoes.*
- *Use swede instead of carrots.*
- *Use chopped fresh parsley or mixed herbs instead of chives.*

tomato *and* basil penne

Freshly cooked pasta served with a delicious tomato sauce makes a quick, delicious meal. The complex carbohydrates found in pasta may increase levels of serotonin, a chemical known for its calming properties. Serotonin can also help ease anxiety and increase the ability to wind down.

ingredients

- 1tbsp olive oil
- 6 shallots (French shallots), finely chopped
- 2 cloves garlic, finely chopped
- 2 sticks celery, finely chopped
- 700g (1lb 9oz) tomatoes, skinned seeded and chopped
- 4 sun-dried tomatoes, soaked, drained and finely chopped
- 2tbsp medium-dry sherry
- 1tbsp tomato purée (paste)
- ½tsp light brown sugar
- sea salt
- freshly ground black pepper
- 350g (12oz) penne
- 2–3tbsp chopped fresh basil
- freshly grated Parmesan cheese, to serve
- fresh basil sprigs, to garnish

serves *four*
preparation time *15 minutes*
cooking time *30–35 minutes*

method

1 Heat the oil in a saucepan, add the shallots, garlic and celery, and cook gently for 5 minutes, stirring occasionally, until soft.

2 Add the tomatoes, sun-dried tomatoes, sherry, tomato purée, sugar and seasoning, and mix well. Cover, bring to the boil, then reduce the heat and simmer for 15 minutes, stirring occasionally.

3 Uncover, increase the heat slightly and cook for a further 10–15 minutes, until the mixture is cooked and thickened.

4 Meanwhile, cook the pasta until just cooked or *al dente*.

5 Drain the pasta well, then toss the pasta, tomato sauce and chopped basil together.

6 Serve hot, sprinkled with a little Parmesan cheese and garnished with the basil sprigs.

7 Serve with a mixed dark-green leaf salad.

variations

- *Use 1 leek instead of shallots.*
- *Use carrots instead of celery.*
- *Use chopped fresh mixed herbs instead of basil.*

raspberry *and* apple oatmeal crumble

This fruit crumble is good served with home-made custard, a little crème fraîche or light sour cream. Fresh fruits such as raspberries and apples are a good source of vitamin C, a vital vitamin for anyone suffering from stress.

ingredients

- 115g (4oz) plain wholemeal flour
- 85g (3oz) fine oatmeal
- 85g (3oz) butter, chopped
- 115g (4oz) light brown sugar
- 225g (8oz) fresh raspberries
- 225g (8oz) eating apples (peeled and cored weight), thinly sliced
- 1tsp ground cinnamon

serves *four*
preparation time *15 minutes*
cooking time *45 minutes*

method

1 Preheat the oven to 180°C/350°F/gas mark 4.
2 Mix the flour and oatmeal in a bowl, then rub in the butter until the mixture resembles breadcrumbs. Stir in 85g (3oz) of the brown sugar.
3 Put the raspberries and apples in an ovenproof dish. Mix the remaining sugar and cinnamon, and sprinkle over the fruit.
4 Spoon the oatmeal mixture evenly over the fruit.
5 Bake for about 45 minutes, until the fruit is cooked and the topping is golden brown.
6 Serve hot or cold with home-made custard, crème fraîche or light sour cream.

variations

- *Use other combinations of fresh fruits, such as peaches and raspberries, apples and pears, or apricots and pineapple.*
- *Use ground mixed spice or ginger instead of cinnamon.*

freezing instructions

Allow to cool completely, then transfer to a rigid, freezeproof container. Cover, seal and label. Freeze for up to 3 months. Defrost, and reheat in a moderate oven until piping hot.

date *and* raisin flapjacks

These chewy, fruity flapjack bars are ideal for a packed lunch. Oats help the body produce the calming hormone serotonin. Dried fruit contains iron and magnesium.

ingredients

- 115g (4oz) butter
- 85g (3oz) light brown sugar
- 3tbsp maple syrup
- 85g (3oz) rolled oats
- 85g (3oz) sugar-free Swiss-style muesli
- 55g (2oz) dried dates, finely chopped
- 55g (2oz) raisins

makes *eight to ten bars*
preparation time *15 minutes*
cooking time *20–30 minutes*

method

1 Preheat the oven to 180°C/350°F/gas mark 4.
2 Lightly grease a shallow, 18cm (7in) square cake tin.
3 Put the butter, sugar and syrup in a saucepan and heat gently until melted. Remove from the heat.
4 Stir in the oats, muesli, dates and raisins, and mix well.
5 Transfer the mixture to the prepared tin, pressing it down well to level the surface.
6 Bake for 20–30 minutes, until pale golden brown. Mark into fingers or squares while still warm, then allow to cool completely in the tin.
7 When cool, break into fingers or squares.

variations

- *Use honey instead of maple syrup.*
- *Use ready-to-eat dried apricots and apples instead of dates and raisins.*
- *Add 1tsp ground mixed spice, ginger or cinnamon to the mixture before baking.*

fruit salad *with* ginger

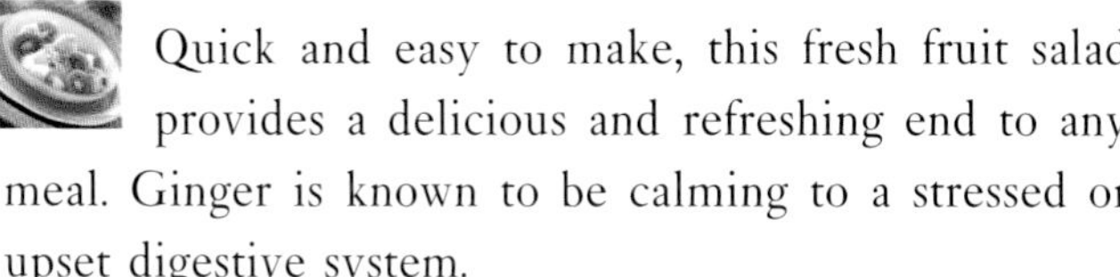

Quick and easy to make, this fresh fruit salad provides a delicious and refreshing end to any meal. Ginger is known to be calming to a stressed or upset digestive system.

ingredients

- 1 small melon
- 6 kiwifruit
- 25g (1oz) preserved stem ginger in syrup, drained
- 200ml (7fl oz) unsweetened apple juice
- 100ml (3½fl oz) unsweetened white grape juice
- 2tbsp ginger wine
- fresh mint sprigs, to decorate

serves *four*
preparation time *15 minutes, plus 1 hour standing time*

method

1 Halve the melon and discard the seeds. Peel the melon, dice the flesh and place it in a bowl.
2 Peel and slice the kiwifruit and finely chop the stem ginger. Add to the bowl and stir.
3 Mix the fruit juices and ginger wine and pour over the fruit. Stir, then cover and leave to stand at room temperature for 1 hour before serving to allow the flavours to blend.
4 Decorate with the mint sprigs and serve with a little crème fraîche, light sour cream or plain yoghurt.

variations

- *Use 1 small fresh pineapple instead of the melon.*
- *Use a mixture of unsweetened orange and pineapple juices instead of the apple and grape juices.*
- *Use brandy or sherry instead of ginger wine.*

easy like sunday morning

SIT BACK AND RELAX *with this selection of recipes from the relaxing foods section. These recipes are rich in nutrients that increase levels of the stress-busting and tranquilising hormones serotonin and tryptophan. So settle down to a nutritious feast that will calm and soothe away the strain of the day.*

green salad *with* avocado dressing

A fabulous mind soother, this salad contains a whole host of vitamins and minerals to help improve your mental state.

ingredients

- 140g (5oz) mixed dark-green salad leaves, such as baby spinach, lollo rosso (coral lettuce), red (ruby) chard and rocket
- 55g (2oz) watercress
- 1 green pepper (capsicum), seeded and sliced
- half a cucumber, thinly sliced
- 6–8 spring onions, chopped
- 55–85g (2–3oz) walnuts, roughly chopped

for the dressing

- 1 large avocado
- finely grated rind and juice of 1 lemon
- 6tbsp plain yoghurt
- 1tsp Dijon mustard
- sea salt
- freshly ground black pepper

serves *four to six*
preparation time *15 minutes*

method

1 Put the salad leaves in a large bowl. Add the watercress, green pepper, cucumber and spring onions, and toss together. Divide the salad among four or six serving plates or bowls.
2 To make the dressing, peel, stone and chop the avocado, and place in a food processor with the lemon rind and juice. Purée until smooth. Add the yoghurt, mustard and seasoning, and blend.
3 Spoon some dressing over each salad, sprinkle with the walnuts and serve with crusty wholemeal bread.

salmon, pepper *and* mushroom wholemeal pizza

The B-vitamins in this pizza make this main course an excellent de-stresser.

ingredients

- 1tbsp olive oil
- 4 shallots (French shallots), sliced
- 1 red pepper (capsicum), seeded and sliced
- 225g (8oz) mushrooms, sliced
- 1 clove garlic, crushed
- 4tbsp passata (sieved tomatoes)
- 4 sun-dried tomatoes in oil, drained and finely chopped
- 1–2tbsp chopped fresh mixed herbs
- sea salt
- freshly ground black pepper

- 213g (7½oz) can salmon in water, drained and flaked
- 2 plum (Roma) tomatoes, sliced
- 115g (4oz) Cheddar cheese, grated
- fresh herb sprigs, to garnish

for the pizza base

- 175g (6oz) plain wholemeal flour
- 55g (2oz) fine oatmeal
- pinch of salt
- 2tsp baking powder
- 55g (2oz) butter, chopped
- about 100ml (3½fl oz) milk

serves *four to six*
preparation time *25 minutes*
cooking time *25–30 minutes*

method

1 Preheat the oven to 220°C/425°F/gas mark 7.

2 Line a baking tray with non-stick baking paper.

3 Heat the oil in a saucepan, add the shallots, pepper, mushrooms and garlic. Cook gently for 10 minutes, stirring occasionally, until soft.

4 Meanwhile, make the pizza base. Put the flour, oatmeal, salt and baking powder in a bowl and lightly rub in the butter until the mixture resembles breadcrumbs. Add enough milk to form a soft but not sticky dough.

5 Roll the dough out on a lightly floured surface to a circle roughly 25cm (10in) in diameter. Place the dough on the baking tray and make the edges slightly thicker than the centre.

6 Mix the passata, sun-dried tomatoes, chopped herbs and seasoning together and spread over the pizza base.

7 Spoon the cooked vegetables over the base, scatter over the salmon and top with the tomato slices. Sprinkle the cheese evenly over the top.

8 Bake for 25–30 minutes, until cooked and golden brown.

9 Garnish with the herb sprigs and serve hot or cold with crusty wholemeal bread and a pepper and tomato salad.

raspberry *and* apple oatmeal crumble

Boost your vitamin C levels with the raspberries and apples in this nutritious dessert.

ingredients

- 115g (4oz) plain wholemeal flour
- 85g (3oz) fine oatmeal
- 85g (3oz) butter, chopped
- 115g (4oz) light brown sugar
- 225g (8oz) fresh raspberries
- 225g (8oz) eating apples (peeled and cored weight), thinly sliced
- 1tsp ground cinnamon

serves *four*
preparation time *15 minutes*
cooking time *45 minutes*

method

1 Preheat the oven to 180°C/350°F/gas mark 4.

2 Mix the flour and oatmeal in a bowl, then rub in the butter until the mixture resembles breadcrumbs. Stir in 85g (3oz) of the brown sugar.

3 Put the raspberries and apples in an ovenproof dish. Mix the remaining sugar and cinnamon, and sprinkle over the fruit.

4 Spoon the oatmeal mixture evenly over the fruit.

5 Bake for about 45 minutes, until the fruit is cooked and the topping is golden brown.

6 Serve hot or cold with home-made custard or plain yoghurt.

sensuous *foods*

EATING CAN BE A *sensuous experience and some foods even seem to arouse sensual feelings. The recipes in this section can help lift the spirits and increase alertness. Foods such as apricots, bananas, avocado, green leafy and root vegetables, pulses, nuts, eggs, poultry, oily fish, lamb's liver and kidneys are good sources of B group vitamins that can affect the way we feel.*

goat's cheese *and* spinach salad

This salad is quick and easy to prepare and makes a good starter or snack. Protein foods such as goat's cheese can be stimulating and mentally arousing, and some people say they help lift moods.

ingredients

- 115g (4oz) baby spinach
- 55g (2oz) watercress
- 25g (1oz) alfalfa sprouts
- 115g (4oz) mangetout (snowpeas), chopped
- 250g (9oz) cherry tomatoes, halved
- 4tbsp French dressing (see recipe on page 21)
- sea salt
- freshly ground black pepper
- 225g (8oz) goat's cheese, thinly sliced or diced

serves *four*
preparation time *10 minutes*

method

1 Put the spinach, watercress, alfalfa sprouts, mangetout and tomatoes in a bowl and toss together.
2 Whisk the dressing to ensure it is well mixed and adjust the seasoning if necessary. Drizzle over the salad vegetables and toss.
3 Divide the salad among four plates and scatter some goat's cheese over the top.
4 Serve immediately with wholemeal bread.

variations

- *Use shredded round (butterhead) lettuce leaves instead of watercress.*
- *Use rocket instead of alfalfa sprouts.*

fresh mushroom soup

Mushrooms and parsley contain B vitamins and iron. Deficiencies of these nutrients can result in impaired brain function.

ingredients

- 25g (1oz) butter
- 1 onion, chopped
- 350g (12oz) mushrooms, sliced
- 300ml (½ pint) vegetable stock (see recipe on page 20)
- 300ml (½ pint) milk
- sea salt
- freshly ground black pepper
- 1–2tbsp chopped fresh parsley
- fresh parsley sprigs, to garnish

serves *four*
preparation time *10 minutes*
cooking time *25–30 minutes*

method

1 Melt the butter in a large saucepan, add the onion and cook gently for 3 minutes.
2 Add the mushrooms and cook gently for 5 minutes.
3 Stir in the stock, milk and seasoning, then cover and bring to the boil. Reduce the heat and simmer for 15–20 minutes until the vegetables are cooked and tender, stirring occasionally.
4 Remove the pan from the heat and allow to cool slightly, then purée in a food processor.
5 Return the soup to the rinsed-out saucepan, stir in the chopped parsley, then reheat gently until piping hot, stirring occasionally.
6 Ladle into warmed soup bowls, garnish with the parsley sprigs and serve with wholemeal rolls.

variation

- *Use 2 leeks instead of the onion.*

chicken *and* asparagus frittata

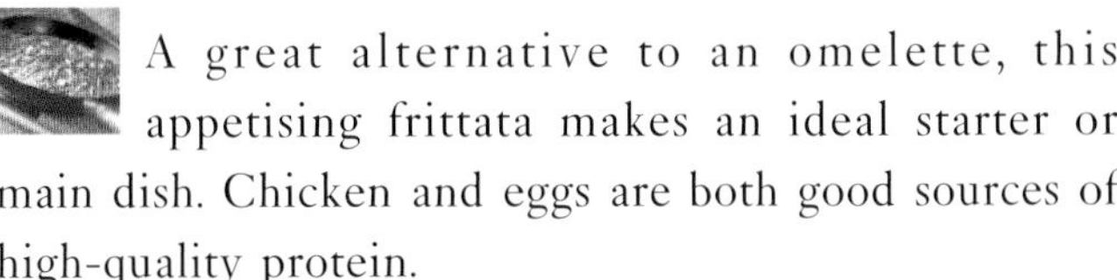

A great alternative to an omelette, this appetising frittata makes an ideal starter or main dish. Chicken and eggs are both good sources of high-quality protein.

ingredients

- 115g (4oz) asparagus tips
- 2tbsp olive oil
- 115g (4oz) courgettes (zucchini), thinly sliced
- 6–8 spring onions, chopped
- 6 medium eggs
- 200g (7oz) can sweetcorn kernels, drained
- 225g (8oz) cooked skinless, boneless chicken breast, diced
- 55g (2oz) Cheddar cheese, grated
- 1tbsp chopped fresh parsley
- 1tbsp chopped fresh tarragon
- sea salt
- freshly ground black pepper
- fresh herb sprigs, to garnish

serves *four to six*
preparation time *10 minutes*
cooking time *25–30 minutes*

method

1 Cook the asparagus in boiling water for 4 minutes. Drain well and keep warm.
2 Heat the oil in a large non-stick frying pan, add the courgettes and spring onions, and cook gently for 5 minutes.
3 Beat the eggs in a bowl, then stir in the asparagus, sweetcorn, chicken, cheese, herbs and seasoning. Pour the egg mixture into the frying pan and stir briefly, spreading the mixture out evenly.
4 Cook until the eggs are beginning to set and the frittata is golden brown underneath.
5 Preheat the grill to medium. Grill the frittata until the top is golden brown.
6 Cut into wedges, garnish with the herb sprigs and serve hot with a mixed dark-green leaf salad.

variations

- *Use mushrooms instead of courgettes.*
- *Use cooked turkey, tuna or salmon instead of chicken.*

tuna *and* prawn savoury flan

This seafood flan makes a nutritious meal served with baked potatoes and a mixed salad. Fish and shellfish contain an amino acid called tyrosine, which is used to make brain-stimulating chemicals that increase mental energy and alertness.

ingredients

for the pastry

- 140g (5oz) plain wholemeal flour
- 25g (1oz) fine oatmeal
- pinch of salt
- 85g (3oz) butter, chopped

for the filling

- 100g (3½oz) can tuna in water, drained and flaked
- 115g (4oz) small cooked, peeled prawns
- 115g (4oz) canned sweetcorn kernels (drained weight)
- 1 tomato, skinned, seeded and chopped
- 2 medium eggs
- 150ml (¼ pint) milk
- 55g (2oz) Cheddar cheese, finely grated
- 1–2tbsp chopped fresh basil
- sea salt and ground black pepper
- fresh herb sprigs, to garnish

serves *four to six*
preparation time *15 minutes, plus 20 minutes' chilling time*
cooking time *55 minutes*

method

1 Preheat the oven to 200°C/400°F/gas mark 6.
2 To make the pastry, put the flour, oatmeal and salt in a bowl, then lightly rub in the butter until the mixture resembles breadcrumbs. Add enough cold water to form a soft dough.
3 Roll the dough out on a lightly floured surface and use to line a 20cm (8in) flan tin. Cover and chill for 20 minutes.
4 Line the pastry case with non-stick baking paper and fill with baking beans. Place on a baking tray and bake blind for about 10 minutes, until firm and lightly brown. Remove from the oven and lift out the paper and beans.
5 Reduce the oven temperature to 180°C/350°F/gas mark 4.
6 Mix the tuna, prawns and sweetcorn together and spoon into the flan case. Scatter with the chopped tomato.
7 Beat the eggs, milk, cheese, basil and seasoning together and pour into the flan case.
8 Bake for about 45 minutes, until lightly set and golden brown.
9 Garnish with the herb sprigs and serve warm or cold with baked potatoes and a mixed salad.

variations

- *Use canned salmon and cooked mussels instead of tuna and prawns.*
- *Use chopped fresh chives or parsley instead of basil.*

freezing instructions

Allow to cool completely, then wrap in foil or seal in a freezer bag and label. Freeze for up to 3 months. Defrost completely, and serve cold or reheat in a moderate oven until piping hot.

grilled lemon sole *with* fresh parsley sauce

Fresh lemon sole fillets served with parsley sauce make a simple but delicious dish. Fresh fish is a good source of protein, magnesium, selenium and B vitamins, all of which are important brain nutrients.

ingredients

- 2tbsp cornflour
- 300ml (½ pint) milk
- 2–3tbsp chopped fresh parsley
- 15g (½oz) butter, chopped
- sea salt
- freshly ground black pepper
- 8 lemon sole (or flounder) fillets
- 2tbsp olive oil
- fresh parsley sprigs, to garnish

serves *four*
preparation time *10 minutes*
cooking time *4–6 minutes*

method

1 Line a grill rack with foil and preheat the grill to medium.

2 In a saucepan, blend the cornflour with a little of the milk. Stir in the remaining milk, then heat gently, stirring continuously, until the sauce comes to the boil and thickens. Simmer gently for 2 minutes, stirring.

3 Add the chopped parsley, butter and seasoning, and heat gently until piping hot, stirring continuously. Keep the sauce hot while cooking the fish.

4 Place the fillets on the grill rack and brush lightly with oil. Grill for 4–6 minutes, until the fish is cooked and the flesh just flakes when tested with a fork, carefully turning over once during cooking.

5 Place two cooked fish fillets on each warmed serving plate. Pour some parsley sauce over the fish and garnish with the parsley sprigs.

6 Serve with cooked fresh vegetables, such as new potatoes, baby (Dutch) carrots and broccoli.

variations

- *Serve the parsley sauce with other cooked white fish.*
- *Use fresh chives instead of parsley.*

turkey breast steaks *with* cranberry sauce

Cranberry sauce is a traditional and delicious accompaniment to turkey. Turkey breasts are especially high in protein.

ingredients

- 225g (8oz) fresh, frozen (defrosted) or canned (drained) cranberries
- 1 eating apple, peeled, cored and finely chopped
- 175g (6oz) light brown sugar
- 1–2tbsp port
- 6 turkey breast steaks, each about 125g (4½oz)
- a little olive oil, for brushing
- sea salt
- freshly ground black pepper
- fresh herb sprigs, to garnish

serves *six*
preparation time *20 minutes*
cooking time *20 minutes*

method

1 To make the sauce, put the cranberries and chopped apple in a saucepan with 150ml (¼ pint) water. Cover, bring to the boil, then reduce the heat and simmer for about 10 minutes, until the fruit is soft. If using canned cranberries, they need only be warmed through.

2 Stir in the sugar (canned cranberries will need a little less), then cook gently until the sugar has dissolved, stirring constantly. Stir in the port and remove the pan from the heat.

3 Preheat the grill to medium. Lightly brush the turkey steaks with oil, then season with salt and pepper. Place the turkey steaks on a rack in a grill pan and grill for about 20 minutes, until cooked and tender, turning once.

4 Serve the turkey with warm or cold cranberry sauce spooned alongside.

5 Garnish with the herb sprigs and serve with oven-baked fresh vegetables and brown rice.

variations

- *Use brandy or sherry instead of port.*
- *Use 1 pear instead of the apple.*

lamb *and* vegetable couscous

This casserole of lamb and vegetables served on a bed of hot couscous will be popular with the whole family. Lamb is high in protein, iron and B group vitamins. The complex carbohydrates in couscous may increase the level of serotonin, a brain chemical that helps you feel calmer and more relaxed.

ingredients

- 1tbsp olive oil
- 350g (12oz) lean lamb fillet, cut into 2.5cm (1in) cubes
- 1 onion, sliced
- 1 large clove garlic, chopped
- 1 green pepper (capsicum), seeded and sliced
- 3 sticks celery, chopped
- 3 carrots, thinly sliced
- 225g (8oz) baby new potatoes
- 1tsp each ground cumin, ground coriander and hot chilli powder
- 400g (14oz) can tomatoes, chopped
- 150ml (¼ pint) vegetable stock (see recipe on page 20)
- sea salt and black pepper
- 175g (6oz) cauliflower florets
- 350g (12oz) quick-cook (instant) couscous
- 25g (1oz) butter
- fresh herb sprigs, to garnish

serves *four*
preparation time *15 minutes*
cooking time *about 1 hour*

method

1 Heat the oil in a large saucepan, add the lamb and cook until brown all over, stirring occasionally.
2 Add the onion and garlic, and cook gently for 3 minutes.
3 Add the green pepper, celery, carrots, new potatoes and ground spices, and cook for 1 minute, stirring.
4 Stir in the tomatoes, stock and seasoning. Cover, bring to the boil, reduce the heat and simmer for 30 minutes, stirring occasionally.
5 Stir in the cauliflower, then cover and simmer for a further 30–45 minutes, until the lamb and vegetables are cooked and tender, stirring occasionally.
6 Meanwhile, cook the couscous according to the instructions on the packet.
7 Stir the butter into the hot couscous, then spoon it onto warmed serving plates. Spoon the lamb and vegetables on top and serve garnished with the herb sprigs.

variations

- *Thicken the sauce with a little cornflour before serving. Blend 1tbsp cornflour with 2tbsp water. Stir into the cooked lamb and vegetable sauce and bring to the boil, stirring continuously. Simmer gently for 2 minutes, stirring, then serve.*
- *Use skinless, boneless chicken or turkey instead of lamb.*
- *Use parsnips instead of carrots.*

freezing instructions

The sauce can be frozen. Allow to cool completely, then transfer to a rigid, freezeproof container. Cover, seal and label. Freeze for up to 3 months. Defrost completely, and reheat gently in a saucepan until hot.

baked red cabbage *with* apples

Oven-baked red cabbage can be served with baked potatoes and cheese – or it makes a delicious accompaniment to grilled lean meat or fish. Cabbage is a good source of vitamin C and some of the B group vitamins.

ingredients

- 450g (1lb) red cabbage, shredded
- 2 eating apples, peeled, cored and sliced
- 6 shallots (French shallots), thinly sliced
- 1 clove garlic, crushed
- 2tbsp unsweetened apple juice
- 2tsp honey
- 2tsp red wine vinegar
- sea salt
- freshly ground black pepper
- 15g (½oz) butter
- 25–55g (1–2oz) pine nuts, toasted (optional)
- fresh herb sprigs, to garnish

serves *four as an accompaniment*
preparation time *10 minutes*
cooking time *1–1½ hours*

method

1 Preheat the oven to 190°C/375°F/gas mark 5.

2 Put the cabbage, apples, shallots, garlic, apple juice, honey, vinegar and seasoning in an ovenproof casserole dish and mix well. Cover and bake for 1–1½ hours, until the vegetables are cooked and tender, stirring once or twice.

3 Stir in the butter and pine nuts, if using, and serve garnished with the herb sprigs.

4 Serve with oven-baked potatoes topped with a little grated Cheddar cheese or diced goat's cheese.

variations

- *Use 1 onion instead of shallots.*
- *Use unsweetened grape juice or medium cider instead of apple juice.*
- *Use flaked or chopped almonds instead of pine nuts.*

harvest vegetable hotpot

This nutritious vegetable hotpot makes a delicious dish for chilly evenings. Fresh vegetables are a good source of B group vitamins and vitamin C, which are good for the healthy functioning of the brain and nervous system.

ingredients

- 450g (1lb) potatoes, thinly sliced
- 2tbsp olive oil
- 225g (8oz) baby (pickling) onions or shallots (French shallots)
- 1 clove garlic, crushed
- 2 sticks celery, chopped
- 225g (8oz) carrots, thinly sliced
- 225g (8oz) swede, diced
- 225g (8oz) parsnips, diced
- 225g (8oz) small cauliflower florets
- 400g (14oz) can tomatoes, chopped
- 300ml (½ pint) vegetable stock (see recipe on page 20)
- 150ml (¼ pint) dry white wine
- 2tsp dried *herbes de provence*
- sea salt
- freshly ground black pepper
- 1tbsp cornflour
- fresh herb sprigs, to garnish

serves *four to six*
preparation time *30 minutes*
cooking time *1 hour*

method

1 Preheat the oven to 200°C/400°F/gas mark 6.

2 Parboil the potatoes in boiling water for 4 minutes, then drain. Toss in 1tbsp oil.

3 Heat the remaining oil in a large saucepan, add the onions or shallots, garlic and celery, and cook for 3 minutes, stirring constantly.

4 Add the remaining vegetables, stock, wine, dried herbs and seasoning, and mix well.

5 Blend the cornflour with 2tbsp water and stir into the vegetables. Bring to the boil, stirring constantly, until the mixture thickens.

6 Transfer the vegetables to an ovenproof dish. Arrange the potato slices over the top. Cover with foil and bake for about 1 hour, until tender. Remove the foil for the last 20 minutes.

7 Garnish with the herb sprigs.

variations

- *Use sweet potatoes instead of standard potatoes.*
- *Use celeriac instead of swede.*

curried tofu *and* broad bean salad

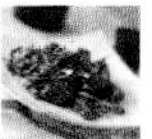

Lightly grilled tofu is combined with fresh vegetables and a tasty dressing to make this flavoursome dish. Tofu is a good source of magnesium and calcium, which are important nutrients for a healthy nervous system.

ingredients

- 350g (12oz) tofu, cut into 2.5cm (1in) cubes
- 3tbsp olive oil
- 1½tsp ground coriander
- 1½tsp ground cumin
- 1tsp hot chilli powder
- 1tsp ground turmeric
- sea salt
- freshly ground black pepper
- 225g (8oz) frozen broad beans
- 225g (8oz) green beans, cut into 5cm (2in) lengths
- 115g (4oz) round (butterhead) lettuce, shredded
- 6–8 spring onions, chopped

for the dressing

- 6tbsp tomato juice
- 2tsp balsamic vinegar
- 1tsp Dijon mustard
- 1 clove garlic, crushed
- 15ml (1tbsp) chopped fresh basil

serves ***four***
preparation time *25 minutes, plus 30 minutes marinating time*
cooking time *6–8 minutes*

method

1 Thread the tofu pieces onto long skewers.
2 In a small bowl, mix together the oil, ground spices and seasoning. Brush the oil mixture all over the tofu, place the skewers on a plate, cover and set aside for 30 minutes.
3 Cook the broad beans and green beans in boiling water for 4–5 minutes, until tender. Drain, rinse under cold running water, then drain thoroughly and set aside to cool.
4 Put the lettuce and spring onions in a bowl, add the cooled beans and toss.
5 Put the tomato juice, vinegar, mustard, garlic, basil and seasoning in a small bowl and whisk until thoroughly mixed.
6 Drizzle the dressing over the salad and toss together. Set aside.
7 Preheat the grill to high. Place the tofu skewers on a rack in a grill pan and grill for 3–4 minutes on each side, until lightly browned.
8 Remove the tofu from the skewers, add to the bean salad and toss lightly.
9 Serve immediately with oatcakes, crispbread or crusty wholemeal bread.

variations

- *Use 1–2tbsp curry powder or curry paste instead of ground spices.*
- *Use canned (drained) sweetcorn kernels instead of green beans. Do not cook the sweetcorn.*

hazelnut meringues

These meringues, sandwiched together with crème fraîche make an irresistible dessert. Hazelnuts contain B vitamins, boron and iron.

ingredients

- 3 medium egg whites
- 175g (6oz) light brown sugar
- 55g (2oz) toasted hazelnuts, ground or finely chopped
- ½tsp ground cinnamon
- 150g (5½oz) crème fraîche or light sour cream
- 225g (8oz) small strawberries, halved
- 2 kiwifruit, peeled and sliced
- fresh mint sprigs, to decorate

serves *four (makes 8 pairs of meringues)*
preparation time *20 minutes*
cooking time *2–3 hours*

method

1 Preheat the oven to 110°C/225°F/gas mark ¼.
2 Line two baking trays with non-stick baking paper.
3 Put the egg whites in a bowl and whisk until stiff. Gradually whisk in the sugar, until the egg whites are stiff and shiny.
4 Gently fold in the hazelnuts and ground cinnamon.
5 Spoon the meringue mixture onto the baking trays to make 16 small mounds. Bake for 2–3 hours until firm and crisp. Transfer to a wire rack to cool, then carefully peel off the paper.
6 Sandwich pairs of meringues with the crème fraîche or light sour cream.
7 Serve with strawberry halves and kiwi slices. Decorate with the mint sprigs.

variations

- *Use almonds instead of hazelnuts.*
- *Use a few drops of vanilla or almond essence instead of cinnamon.*

peach *and* banana fool

This delicious fool is ideal for a quick and nutritious family dessert. Yoghurt is a protein food, containing chemicals to stimulate and arouse the mind. Bananas are a good source of vitamin B_6.

ingredients

- 410g (14oz) can peaches in fruit juice, drained
- 2 bananas, peeled, sliced and tossed in a little lemon juice
- 2tbsp honey
- 1tsp ground ginger
- 250g (9oz) plain yoghurt
- 140g (5oz) crème fraîche or light sour cream
- 25g (1oz) toasted flaked almonds, to decorate

serves *six*
preparation time *10 minutes, plus 30 minutes chilling time*

method

1 Put the peaches, bananas, honey and ginger in a blender or food processor and blend until smooth. Transfer the mixture to a bowl.
2 Fold the yoghurt and crème fraîche or light sour cream into the fruit mixture, mixing well.
3 Spoon into serving glasses or dishes and refrigerate for 30 minutes before serving.
4 Sprinkle flaked almonds over the top before serving.
5 Serve with home-made oat or wholemeal biscuits.

variations

- *Use canned apricots or pears instead of peaches.*
- *Use ground cinnamon or nutmeg instead of ginger.*

fruity florentines

These florentines made of mixed fruit, nuts and seeds are wonderful for a packed lunch or snack. Chocolate can be wonderfully calming and soothing, and makes us feel good.

ingredients

- 55g (2oz) butter
- 55g (2oz) light brown sugar
- 1tbsp maple syrup
- 25g (1oz) plain wholemeal flour
- 85g (3oz) mixed dried fruit, including sultanas, raisins and chopped, ready-to-eat dried apricots
- 55g (2oz) mixed nuts, including walnuts, hazelnuts and almonds, roughly chopped
- 25g (1oz) mixed sunflower and pumpkin seeds
- 115g (4oz) plain (dark) chocolate, broken into squares

makes *12–14*
preparation time *20 minutes*
cooking time *10–15 minutes*

method

1 Preheat the oven to 170°C/325°F/gas mark 3.

2 Line 2 large baking trays with non-stick baking paper.

3 Put the butter, sugar and syrup in a saucepan and heat gently until melted, stirring constantly.

4 Remove the pan from the heat, then stir in the flour, dried fruit, nuts and seeds.

5 Drop teaspoonfuls of the mixture onto the baking trays, allowing room between each one for spreading.

6 Bake for 10–15 minutes, until golden brown. Remove from the oven and immediately push in the edges of the florentines with a non-stick palette knife to neaten the round shapes. Leave on the baking trays for a few minutes to firm up slightly, then transfer to a wire rack to cool completely.

7 Put the chocolate in a bowl over a saucepan of simmering water and stir until melted. Remove from the heat.

8 Spread some chocolate over the smooth side of each biscuit, then place on a wire rack, chocolate-side up, and allow to set completely before serving.

variations

- *For a tasty dessert, serve the florentines with fresh fruit, such as strawberries and raspberries, and a little plain yoghurt, crème fraîche or light sour cream.*
- *Use honey instead of maple syrup.*

dinner for two

SMOOTH AWAY YOUR *lover's furrowed brow and get into a relaxing, seductive mood with this deliciously arousing menu. These recipes will provide you with enough energy for a night of passion. The protein and carbohydrates will help to increase the level of soothing hormones.*

goat's cheese *and* spinach salad

This sensuous salad could help chase away the blues and lighten your mood.

ingredients

- 115g (4oz) baby spinach
- 55g (2oz) watercress
- 25g (1oz) alfalfa sprouts
- 115g (4oz) mangetout (snowpeas), chopped
- 250g (9oz) cherry tomatoes, halved
- 4tbsp French dressing (see recipe on page 21)
- sea salt
- freshly ground black pepper
- 225g (8oz) goat's cheese, thinly sliced or diced

serves *four*
preparation time *10 minutes*

method

1 Put the spinach, watercress, alfalfa sprouts, mangetout and tomatoes in a bowl and toss together.
2 Whisk the dressing to ensure it is well mixed and adjust the seasoning if necessary. Drizzle over the salad vegetables and toss.
3 Divide the salad among four plates and scatter some goat's cheese over the top.
4 Serve immediately with wholemeal bread.

lamb *and* vegetable couscous

Lamb provides mentally arousing protein, and the complex carbohydrates in the couscous help to increase the brain's level of soothing serotonin.

ingredients

- 1tbsp olive oil
- 350g (12oz) lean lamb fillet, cut into 2.5cm (1in) cubes
- 1 onion, sliced
- 1 large clove garlic, chopped
- 1 green pepper (capsicum), seeded and sliced
- 3 sticks celery, chopped
- 3 carrots, thinly sliced
- 225g (8oz) baby new potatoes
- 1tsp each ground cumin, ground coriander and hot chilli powder
- 400g (14oz) can tomatoes, chopped
- 150ml (¼ pint) vegetable stock (see recipe on page 20)
- sea salt and black pepper
- 175g (6oz) cauliflower florets
- 350g (12oz) quick-cook (instant) couscous
- 25g (1oz) butter
- fresh herb sprigs, to garnish

serves *four*
preparation time *15 minutes*
cooking time *about 1 hour*

method

1 Heat the oil in a large saucepan, add the lamb and cook until brown all over, stirring occasionally.
2 Add the onion and garlic, and cook gently for 3 minutes.
3 Add the green pepper, celery, carrots, new potatoes and ground spices, and cook for 1 minute, stirring.
4 Stir in the tomatoes, stock and seasoning. Cover, bring to the boil, reduce the heat and simmer for 30 minutes, stirring occasionally.
5 Stir in the cauliflower, then cover and simmer for a further 30–45 minutes, until the lamb and vegetables are cooked and tender, stirring occasionally.
6 Meanwhile, cook the couscous according to the instructions on the packet.
7 Stir the butter into the hot couscous, then spoon it onto warmed serving plates. Spoon the lamb and vegetables on top and serve garnished with the herb sprigs.

peach *and* banana fool

The yoghurt in this fool contains tryptophan to soothe and arouse a tired mind.

ingredients

- 410g (14oz) can peaches in fruit juice, drained
- 2 bananas, peeled, sliced and tossed in a little lemon juice
- 2tbsp honey
- 1tsp ground ginger
- 250g (9oz) plain yoghurt
- 140g (5oz) crème fraîche or light sour cream
- 25g (1oz) toasted flaked almonds, to decorate

serves *six*
preparation time *10 minutes, plus 30 minutes chilling time*

method

1 Put the peaches, bananas, honey and ginger in a blender or food processor and blend until smooth. Transfer the mixture to a bowl.
2 Fold the yoghurt and crème fraîche or light sour cream into the fruit mixture, mixing well.
3 Spoon into serving glasses or dishes and refrigerate for 30 minutes before serving.
4 Sprinkle flaked almonds over the top before serving.
5 Serve with home-made oat or wholemeal biscuits.

feel-good *foods*

IF YOU NEED to be wide awake and in top form, eat protein foods as part of a balanced meal for breakfast and lunch. Eggs, yoghurt, cheese, fresh fish, all kinds of beans, chicken and lean meat are all first-class sources of protein.

Extra supplies of vitamin C are important when it comes to helping the body cope when under stress. Nearly all fruits and vegetables contain some vitamin C, but good sources are citrus fruits, apricots, peppers (capsicums), kiwifruit and green leafy vegetables.

mixed leaf *and* toasted nut salad

This simple salad is quick to prepare and makes a nutritious starter or snack. Almonds and hazelnuts supply B vitamins, magnesium, iron and essential fatty acids, all of which are important for a healthy brain and nervous system.

ingredients

- 55g (2oz) whole blanched hazelnuts
- 55g (2oz) whole blanched almonds
- 55g (2oz) pine nuts
- 125g (4½oz) mixed salad leaves, such as lollo rosso (coral lettuce), watercress and spinach.
- 55g (2oz) rocket
- 115g (4oz) mangetout (snowpeas), chopped
- 6tbsp French dressing (see recipe on page 21)

serves *four*
preparation time *15 minutes*
cooking time *3–5 minutes*

method

1 Preheat the grill to medium. Spread the hazelnuts, almonds and pine nuts out on a baking tray. Grill for a few minutes, turning frequently, until lightly browned. Cool, then chop roughly.

2 Put the salad leaves, rocket and mangetout in a large bowl and toss. Divide the salad among four serving plates or bowls and scatter some nuts over the top.

3 Drizzle a little dressing over each salad. Toss lightly and serve with wholemeal bread.

variations

- *Use walnuts and cashew nuts instead of hazelnuts and almonds.*
- *Use rocket instead of watercress.*
- *Whisk 1tsp finely grated lemon rind into the French dressing before serving.*

pink grapefruit *with* cinnamon

Juicy grapefruit, sprinkled with a little sugar and cinnamon and lightly grilled, makes a refreshing starter. Fresh fruit is a good source of vitamin C, and is especially good for when you are feeling stressed.

ingredients

- 2 pink grapefruit
- 2tbsp light brown sugar
- 1–2tsp ground cinnamon
- fresh mint sprigs, to garnish (optional)

serves ***four***
preparation time *10 minutes*
cooking time *3–5 minutes*

method

1 Preheat the grill to medium. Cut each grapefruit in half, then cut between the segments to loosen the flesh.

2 Mix the sugar and cinnamon together and sprinkle over the grapefruit.

3 Place the grapefruit on a rack in a grill pan and grill for a few minutes, until the sugar has melted and the grapefruit are hot.

4 Serve immediately, garnished with the mint sprigs, if liked.

variations

- *Use standard white grapefruit instead of pink grapefruit.*
- *Use ground mixed spice or ginger instead of cinnamon.*
- *Use honey instead of sugar.*

grilled scallop *and* oyster brochettes

These delicious seafood brochettes are an ideal summertime dish, perfect for barbecues. Seafood and shellfish contain zinc and also tyrosine, an amino acid used to make brain-stimulating chemicals that increase mental alertness.

ingredients

- 16 medium or large shelled raw scallops
- 16 shelled raw oysters
- 16 shelled raw tiger (or king) prawns
- 2 small yellow peppers (capsicums), seeded and each cut into 8 pieces
- 1 courgette (zucchini), cut into 16 thin slices
- 16 small ready-to-eat dried apricots
- 4tbsp olive oil
- 2tbsp unsweetened apple juice
- 1 clove garlic, crushed
- 2tbsp chopped fresh mixed herbs
- sea salt
- freshly ground black pepper

serves *four*
preparation time *10 minutes, plus 1 hour for marination*
cooking time *8–10 minutes*

method

1 Thread the scallops, oysters, prawns, vegetables and apricots on to four long skewers, dividing the ingredients evenly between them. Place the skewers in a shallow, non-metallic dish.

2 Put the oil, apple juice, garlic, herbs and seasoning in a small bowl and whisk until thoroughly mixed. Drizzle over the brochettes, then turn the brochettes over in the marinade to coat them completely. Cover and leave to marinate in the refrigerator for 1 hour.

3 Preheat the grill to high. Place the brochettes on a rack in a grill pan and grill for 8–10 minutes, until cooked, turning occasionally. Brush frequently with the marinade during cooking, to prevent the brochettes drying out.

4 Serve with cooked fresh vegetables, such as new potatoes, courgettes (zucchini) and sweetcorn.

variations

- *Use mushrooms instead of apricots.*
- *Use unsweetened orange juice or white grape juice instead of apple.*
- *Use chopped fresh flatleaf parsley instead of mixed herbs.*

sardines *with* sweet pepper *and* lime sauce

Sardines are delicious served with a pepper (capsicum) and lime sauce. Fresh oily fish such as sardines contain omega-3 fatty acids, which are important for the production of healthy brain cells and tissue.

ingredients

- 3tbsp olive oil
- 2 large red peppers (capsicums), seeded and sliced
- 2 shallots (French shallots), finely chopped
- finely grated rind and juice of 1 lime
- 6tbsp tomato juice
- 2tbsp chopped, fresh flatleaf parsley
- sea salt
- freshly ground black pepper
- 700g (1lb 9oz) large sardines, gutted and cleaned
- juice of 1 small lemon
- fresh flatleaf parsley sprigs, to garnish

serves *four*
preparation time *25 minutes*
cooking time *8–14 minutes*

method

1 Heat 2tbsp oil in a saucepan, add the peppers and shallots, and cook for 10–15 minutes, until soft, stirring occasionally.
2 Put the pepper mixture in a food processor with the lime rind and juice, tomato juice, parsley and seasoning, and blend until smooth.
3 Press the purée through a sieve and discard the pulp. Set aside.
4 Preheat the grill to high. Cover a grill rack with foil and put the sardines on the rack.
5 Put the remaining oil, lemon juice and seasoning in a bowl and mix thoroughly. Lightly brush the sardines all over with the oil mixture.
6 Grill the sardines for about 4–7 minutes on each side, until they are cooked, turning once.
7 Serve the sardines with a little pepper sauce drizzled over or spooned alongside.
8 Garnish with the parsley sprigs and serve with sautéed potatoes and a mixed green salad.

variations

- *Add 1 small crushed clove of garlic to the sauce.*
- *Use fresh basil instead of parsley.*
- *Chill the sauce before serving.*

lamb cutlets *with* caper sauce

Grilled lamb cutlets with caper sauce make a flavoursome dish for a main meal. Lamb is a high-protein food that also provides iron and B vitamins. Rosemary is said to stimulate the nervous and circulatory systems.

ingredients

- 8 lean lamb cutlets
- 1tbsp chopped fresh rosemary
- fresh rosemary sprigs, to garnish

for the sauce

- 2tbsp cornflour
- 300ml (½ pint) milk
- 2–3tbsp capers, chopped
- 1tbsp vinegar from the jar of capers
- 15g (½oz) butter
- sea salt
- freshly ground black pepper

serves *four*
preparation time *10 minutes*
cooking time *8–12 minutes*

method

1 Preheat the grill to high. Place the lamb cutlets on a rack in a grill pan and sprinkle both sides with a little chopped rosemary. Grill for 4–6 minutes on each side, until cooked.

2 Meanwhile, make the sauce. In a saucepan, blend the cornflour with a little of the milk. Stir in the remaining milk, then heat gently, stirring constantly, until the sauce comes to the boil and thickens.

3 Stir in the capers, vinegar, butter and seasoning, and heat gently until piping hot, stirring continuously.

4 Serve the cutlets with the caper sauce poured over. Garnish with the rosemary sprigs and serve with cooked fresh vegetables, such as potatoes, broccoli and cauliflower.

variations

- *Use green peppercorns bottled in brine (drained) instead of capers.*
- *Use chopped fresh parsley instead of capers.*
- *Serve the caper sauce with other cooked lean meats, such as chicken and turkey.*

chicken breasts stuffed *with* mushrooms *and* sage

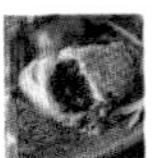

This tasty way of serving chicken is sure to be popular with the whole family. Fresh sage is considered to be a mild stimulant.

ingredients

- 15g (½oz) butter
- 4 shallots (French shallots), finely chopped
- 1 clove garlic, crushed
- 1 small leek, finely chopped
- 115g (4oz) mushrooms, finely chopped
- 1tbsp chopped fresh sage
- 1tsp finely grated lemon rind
- sea salt
- freshly ground black pepper
- 4 large skinless, boneless chicken breasts
- 2tbsp olive oil
- fresh sage leaves, to garnish

serves *four*
preparation time *30 minutes*
cooking time *30–45 minutes*

method

1 Preheat the oven to 200°C/400°F/gas mark 6.
2 Lightly grease a baking tray.
3 Melt the butter in a saucepan. Add the shallots, garlic, leek and mushrooms, and cook gently for about 10 minutes, stirring occasionally, until softened.
4 Remove the pan from the heat. Stir in the chopped sage, lemon rind and seasoning.
5 Place the chicken breasts on a flat surface, cover loosely with a sheet of greaseproof paper and pound with a rolling pin to an even thickness. Remove and discard the paper.
6 Spoon some mushroom mixture across the centre of each breast, then fold one end over the filling and overlap the other end over the top to make a parcel. Secure with cocktail sticks, brush the chicken all over with oil and place, seam-side down, on the baking tray.
7 Bake for 30–45 minutes, until the chicken is cooked through and tender. Remove the cocktail sticks before serving.
8 Garnish with the sage leaves and serve with brown rice and cooked fresh vegetables, such as spinach and swede.

variations

- *Use turkey instead of chicken.*
- *Use fresh thyme instead of sage.*

broad bean *and* parsley bake

This delicious potato-topped bean and vegetable bake makes a good family dish. Parsley is a source of iron and vitamin C, which helps the absorption of iron.

ingredients

- 900g (2lb) potatoes, diced
- knob of butter
- 2tbsp chopped fresh chives
- 450ml (16fl oz) milk, plus 2tbsp
- sea salt
- freshly ground black pepper
- 2 leeks, washed and sliced
- 175g (6oz) mushrooms, sliced
- 350g (12oz) frozen broad beans
- 40g (1½oz) butter
- 40g (1½oz) plain wholemeal flour
- ½tsp English mustard
- 85g (3oz) Cheddar cheese, grated
- 200g (7oz) can sweetcorn kernels, drained
- 3–4tbsp chopped fresh parsley
- fresh parsley sprigs, to garnish

serves *four to six*
preparation time *30 minutes*
cooking time *25–30 minutes*

method

1 Preheat the oven to 190°C/375°F/gas mark 5.
2 Cook the potatoes for 10–15 minutes, until tender. Drain and mash. Stir in the butter, chives, 2tbsp milk and seasoning.
3 Steam the leeks and mushrooms over a saucepan of boiling water for 10 minutes. Add the broad beans and steam for a further 3–5 minutes, until tender.
4 Put the remaining milk, 40g (1½oz) butter, flour and mustard in a saucepan. Heat gently, whisking continuously, until the sauce comes to the boil and thickens. Simmer gently for 3 minutes, stirring.
5 Remove the pan from the heat and stir in the cheese, leeks, mushrooms, broad beans, sweetcorn, parsley and seasoning.
6 Spoon into an ovenproof dish and spoon the potato over the top to cover the bean mixture.
7 Bake for 25–30 minutes, until the potato is crisp.
8 Garnish with parsley sprigs and serve with cooked vegetables.

honey-glazed baby carrots

These delicious, honey-glazed carrots are an ideal accompaniment to grilled lean meat or fish. Carrots are a good source of beta carotene (the plant form of vitamin A) and contain B group vitamins.

ingredients

- 450g (1lb) baby (Dutch) carrots
- 25g (1oz) butter
- 3tbsp honey
- 2tsp chopped fresh thyme
- sea salt
- freshly ground black pepper
- fresh thyme sprigs, to garnish

serves *four as an accompaniment*
preparation time *10 minutes*
cooking time *15–20 minutes*

method

1 Cook the carrots in boiling water for 3 minutes. Drain well and set aside.
2 Put the butter and honey in a saucepan and heat gently until melted. Add the carrots, chopped thyme and seasoning, and mix well. Cover and cook gently for 10–15 minutes, until the carrots are tender and glazed all over, stirring occasionally.
3 Garnish with the thyme sprigs and serve hot with grilled lean meat or fish and minted, boiled new potatoes.

variations

- *Use maple syrup instead of honey.*
- *Use baby sweetcorn instead of carrots.*
- *Serve the carrots with a mixed vegetable pilaf or potato bake, for a vegetarian meal.*

broccoli *and* courgette millet pilaf

Millet pilaf makes a change from rice pilaf and is ideal for a family meal. Millet is a good source of B group vitamins, which are important for healthy brain function. Broccoli contains vitamin C and beta carotene (for vitamin A).

ingredients

- 1tbsp olive oil
- 350g (12oz) shallots (French shallots), chopped
- 1 red pepper (capsicum), seeded and diced
- 1 clove garlic, crushed
- 2 courgettes (zucchini), sliced
- 225g (8oz) millet seed
- 450ml (16fl oz) vegetable stock (see recipe on page 20)
- 150ml (¼ pint) dry white wine
- 115g (4oz) sultanas
- 1tsp ground cinnamon
- sea salt
- freshly ground black pepper
- 280g (10oz) small broccoli florets
- 1–2tbsp chopped fresh mixed herbs
- fresh herb sprigs, to garnish

serves *four to six*
preparation time *10 minutes*
cooking time *20–25 minutes*

method

1 Heat the oil in a large saucepan. Add the shallots, red pepper and garlic, and cook for 5 minutes, stirring occasionally.

2 Add the courgettes, millet, stock, wine, sultanas, cinnamon and seasoning, and mix well. Cover, bring to the boil, then reduce the heat and simmer for 15–20 minutes, until all the liquid has been absorbed and the millet is tender, stirring occasionally.

3 Meanwhile, cook the broccoli in boiling water for about 5 minutes, until cooked. Drain well and keep warm.

4 Fold the broccoli and herbs into the pilaf, garnish with the herb sprigs and serve with a tomato and pepper salad.

variations

- *Use onions instead of shallots.*
- *Use sliced mushrooms or sweetcorn kernels instead of sultanas.*
- *Use chopped ready-to-eat dried apricots instead of sultanas.*

freezing instructions

Allow to cool completely, then transfer to a rigid, freezeproof container. Cover, seal and label. Freeze for up to 3 months. Defrost, and reheat gently in a saucepan until piping hot, adding a little extra stock if necessary.

fresh figs *with* vanilla yoghurt

Enjoy fresh figs when they are at their best, served with vanilla yoghurt. Fresh figs provide small amounts of the many vitamins and minerals necessary for a healthy brain and nervous system.

ingredients

- 200g (7oz) plain yoghurt
- 1–2tbsp honey
- a few drops of vanilla essence
- 8 fresh figs
- finely grated plain (dark) chocolate, for sprinkling (optional)

serves ***four***
preparation time *15 minutes*

method

1 Put the yoghurt, honey and vanilla essence in a bowl and gently fold together. Cover and chill in the refrigerator while preparing the figs.
2 Using a sharp knife, cut the stalk ends off the figs, then cut a deep cross in the top of each fruit. Using your fingers, gently spread each fig open to make four 'petals'.
3 Spoon some vanilla yoghurt into the centre of each fig, or alongside the fruit, and serve immediately, sprinkled with a little grated chocolate, if liked.

variations

- *Use almond essence instead of vanilla essence.*
- *Use maple syrup instead of honey.*
- *Serve the vanilla yoghurt with other prepared fresh fruit, such as passionfruit, nectarines or peaches.*

cherry batter dessert

This fruity, oven-baked cherry batter dessert will be popular with all the family. Cherries contain vitamin C, which the body needs in greater amounts when under stress.

ingredients

- 115g (4oz) plain wholemeal flour
- 55g (2oz) sugar
- 1tsp ground cinnamon
- 1 medium egg
- 300ml (½ pint) milk
- 1tbsp sunflower oil
- 350g (12oz) dark, sweet fresh (pitted) or canned (drained) cherries

serves ***four***
preparation time *15 minutes*
cooking time *25–30 minutes*

method

1 Preheat the oven to 220°C/425°F/gas mark 7.
2 Put the flour, sugar and cinnamon in a bowl, stir, then make a well in the centre. Break in the egg and add a little milk, beating well with a wooden spoon. Gradually beat in the remaining milk, drawing the flour mixture in from the sides, to make a smooth batter.
3 Put the oil in a baking tin 18x28cm (7x11in) and heat in the oven for 2–3 minutes, until hot. Quickly scatter the cherries over the base, then pour the batter evenly over the fruit. Bake for 25–30 minutes, until risen and golden brown.
4 Cut the cherry batter dessert into squares and serve hot or cold, with a little créme fraîche, light sour cream or plain yoghurt

variations

- *Use half wholemeal and half buckwheat flour instead of all wholemeal flour.*
- *Use ginger instead of cinnamon.*

iced terrine of summer fruits

This creamy, iced terrine is an ideal warm weather dessert to enjoy alfresco. Yoghurt is a good source of protein, calcium and B group vitamins.

ingredients

- 450g (1lb) ripe mixed summer fruits, such as strawberries, raspberries, blueberries, blackberries, cherries and redcurrants
- 55g (2oz) light brown sugar
- 280g (10oz) raspberry yoghurt
- 150ml (¼ pint) single (pouring) cream
- 140g (5oz) crème fraîche or light sour cream
- fresh mint sprigs, to decorate

serves *six to eight*
preparation time *20 minutes, plus freezing time*

method

1 Line a 900g (2lb) loaf tin with plastic freezer film and set aside.

2 Put the mixed fruits in a food processor and blend until smooth. Press the purée through a sieve, discarding the seeds and reserving the juice and pulp.

3 Return the fruit pulp and juices to the rinsed-out food processor bowl. Add the sugar, yoghurt, cream and crème fraîche or light sour cream, and blend until well mixed.

4 Pour the mixture into a chilled, shallow, plastic container. Cover and freeze for 1½–2 hours, or until the mixture has a mushy consistency. Spoon into a bowl and mash with a fork to break up the ice crystals.

5 Pour the mixture into the loaf tin and level the surface. Freeze until firm.

6 Turn the terrine out onto a serving plate and peel off and discard the plastic film. Place in the refrigerator for 30 minutes before serving, to soften a little.

7 Decorate with the mint sprigs and serve in slices with fresh fruit, such as apricots and peaches.

variations

- *Use other mixtures of fruits.*
- *Use the same quantity of frozen fruits (defrosted), instead of fresh.*

freezing instructions

This iced terrine will keep for up to 3 months in the freezer.

celebration banquet

DEPRESSED AND WORN *out? Dine your way to tranquillity and happiness – this selection of recipes from the feel-good foods section is an ideal antidote to a stressful day, full of reviving nutrients such as protein and vitamin C. So tuck in to lift your mood!*

pink grapefruit *with* cinnamon

Start off this de-stressing menu with a sweet, vitamin C-rich grapefruit.

ingredients

- 2 pink grapefruit
- 2tbsp light brown sugar
- 1–2tsp ground cinnamon
- fresh mint sprigs, to garnish (optional)

serves *four*
preparation time *10 minutes*
cooking time *3–5 minutes*

method

1 Preheat the grill to medium. Cut each grapefruit in half, then cut between the segments to loosen the flesh.

2 Mix the sugar and cinnamon together and sprinkle over the grapefruit.

3 Place the grapefruit on a rack in a grill pan and grill for a few minutes, until the sugar has melted and the grapefruit are hot.

4 Serve immediately, garnished with the mint sprigs, if liked.

chicken breasts stuffed *with* mushrooms and sage

These chicken breasts are pepped up with sprigs of stimulating sage.

ingredients

- 15g (½oz) butter
- 4 shallots (French shallots), finely chopped
- 1 clove garlic, crushed
- 1 small leek, finely chopped
- 115g (4oz) mushrooms, finely chopped
- 1tbsp chopped fresh sage
- 1tsp finely grated lemon rind
- sea salt
- freshly ground black pepper
- 4 large skinless, boneless chicken breasts
- 2tbsp olive oil
- fresh sage leaves, to garnish

serves *four*
preparation time *30 minutes*
cooking time *30–45 minutes*

method

1 Preheat the oven to 200°C/400°F/gas mark 6.

2 Lightly grease a baking tray.

3 Melt the butter in a saucepan. Add the shallots, garlic, leek and mushrooms, and cook gently for about 10 minutes, stirring occasionally, until softened.

4 Remove the pan from the heat. Stir in the chopped sage, lemon rind and seasoning.

5 Place the chicken breasts on a flat surface, cover loosely with a sheet of greaseproof paper and pound with a rolling pin to an even thickness. Remove and discard the paper.

6 Spoon some mushroom mixture across the centre of each breast, then fold one end over the filling and overlap the other end over the top to make a parcel. Secure with cocktail sticks, brush the chicken all over with oil and place, seam-side down, on the baking tray.

7 Bake for 30–45 minutes, until the chicken is cooked through and tender. Remove the cocktail sticks before serving.

8 Garnish with the sage leaves and serve with brown rice and cooked fresh vegetables, such as spinach and swede.

iced terrine of summer fruits

Yoghurt makes for a protein-rich, soothing and nutritious dessert.

ingredients

- **450g (1lb) ripe mixed summer fruits, such as strawberries, raspberries, blueberries, blackberries, cherries and redcurrants**
- **55g (2oz) light brown sugar**
- **280g (10oz) raspberry yoghurt**
- **150ml (¼ pint) single (pouring) cream**
- **140g (5oz) crème fraîche or light sour cream**
- **fresh mint sprigs, to decorate**

serves *six to eight*
preparation time *20 minutes time*

method

1 Line a 900g (2lb) loaf tin with plastic freezer film and set aside.

2 Put the mixed fruits in a food processor and blend until smooth. Press the purée through a sieve, discarding the seeds and reserving the juice and pulp.

3 Return the fruit pulp and juices to the rinsed-out food processor bowl. Add the sugar, yoghurt, cream and crème fraîche or light sour cream and blend until well mixed.

4 Pour the mixture into a chilled, shallow, plastic container. Cover and freeze for 1½–2 hours, or until the mixture has a mushy consistency. Spoon into a bowl and mash with a fork to break up the ice crystals.

5 Pour the mixture into the loaf tin and level the surface. Freeze until firm.

6 Turn the terrine out onto a serving plate and peel off and discard the plastic film. Place in the refrigerator for 30 minutes before serving, to soften a little.

7 Decorate with the mint sprigs and serve in slices with fresh fruit, such as apricots and peaches.

reviving *foods*

A DEFICIENCY IN MINERALS *can have a profound effect on mood. A lack of calcium and magnesium can cause depression, tenseness and irritability. No one should be short of either of these minerals if they eat plenty of fresh and dried fruit, green and root vegetables, fish, low-fat dairy products, such as yoghurt and cheese, pulses, nuts and seafood. Some areas of the brain have high concentrations of iron, and it is thought that reduced iron levels could also trigger mood changes. Foods that are rich in iron are lean meats, dark-meat poultry, shellfish, fish, green leafy vegetables, dried fruit, nuts and enriched grains.*

green bean vinaigrette

This quick and easy dish makes a good starter or side dish. Green beans contain iron, calcium, magnesium, boron, vitamin C and B group vitamins, important nutrients for a healthy nervous system and brain function.

ingredients

- 700g (1lb 9oz) French (green) beans, trimmed
- 150ml (¼ pint) French dressing (see recipe on page 21)
- 55g (2oz) flaked almonds, toasted

serves *six*
preparation time *10 minutes*
cooking time *5–6 minutes*

method

1 Cook the beans in lightly salted, boiling water for 5–6 minutes, until cooked and tender but still crisp. Drain well.

2 Serve the beans hot or cold, with the French dressing drizzled over the top. Sprinkle with the flaked almonds just before serving.

3 Serve with crusty wholemeal bread or rolls.

variations

- *Use baby (Dutch) carrots or baby sweetcorn instead of beans.*
- *Use chopped, toasted hazelnuts instead of almonds.*
- *Serve the beans as an accompaniment to grilled lean meat or fish with baked potatoes.*

turkey waldorf salad

The addition of turkey brings extra flavour and nutrients to this tasty salad. Walnuts contain essential fatty acids that are especially important for healthy brain tissue and an efficient nervous system.

ingredients

- 6tbsp mayonnaise (see recipe on page 21)
- 4tbsp plain yoghurt
- 2 red-skinned eating apples
- 1tbsp fresh lemon juice
- 225g (8oz) cold, cooked, skinless, boneless turkey breast, diced
- 4 sticks celery, chopped
- 55g (2oz) walnuts, roughly chopped
- 2tbsp chopped fresh chives
- sea salt
- freshly ground black pepper
- 1 round (butterhead) lettuce, shredded
- fresh chives, to garnish

serves *four*
preparation time *15 minutes*

method

1 Mix the mayonnaise and yoghurt in a small bowl and set aside.
2 Core and dice the apples and toss them in the lemon juice.
3 Put the apples in a bowl with the turkey, celery, walnuts and chopped chives, and stir.
4 Add the mayonnaise mixture and toss to mix well. Season to taste with salt and pepper.
5 Arrange the lettuce leaves on a serving plate or platter and spoon the salad on top. Garnish with the chives and serve immediately with wholemeal bread.

variations

- *Use mushrooms instead of turkey.*
- *Use pears instead of apples.*
- *Use pecan or cashew nuts instead of walnuts.*
- *Use cooked chicken breast instead of turkey.*

noodle salad *with* sesame seeds

This warm noodle salad can be served as a filling starter or a snack. Sesame seeds contain iron, magnesium and calcium, all important nutrients for a healthy nervous system.

ingredients

- 4tbsp unsweetened orange juice
- 1tbsp olive oil
- 1tbsp light soy sauce
- 1tbsp red wine vinegar
- 1tbsp honey
- 1tbsp tomato purée (paste)
- 1tbsp dry sherry
- 1 clove garlic, crushed
- sea salt
- freshly ground black pepper
- 250g (9oz) cherry tomatoes, halved
- 85g (3oz) mangetout (snowpeas), chopped
- 85g (3oz) radishes, sliced
- 1 yellow pepper (capsicum), seeded and diced
- 4 spring onions, chopped
- 400g (14oz) can flageolet beans, rinsed and drained
- 175g (6oz) dried egg noodles, broken into short lengths
- 2–3tbsp toasted sesame seeds
- fresh herb sprigs, to garnish

serves *six*
preparation time *15 minutes*
cooking time *4 minutes*

method

1 Put the orange juice, oil, soy sauce, vinegar, honey, tomato purée, sherry, garlic and seasoning in a small bowl and whisk.
2 Put the tomatoes, mangetout, radishes, yellow pepper, spring onions and flageolet beans in a bowl and stir.
3 Cook the noodles according to the packet instructions. Drain well.
4 Give the dressing a quick whisk, then pour it over the hot noodles and toss.
5 Add the noodles to the vegetables and toss together.
6 Sprinkle with sesame seeds and garnish with the herb sprigs. Serve with wholemeal rolls.

variations

- *Use baby sweetcorn, beansprouts and Chinese leaves (greens) instead of cherry tomatoes, mangetout and radishes.*
- *Use unsweetened white grape juice or apple juice instead of orange juice.*
- *Use canned kidney beans or black-eye beans instead of flageolet beans.*

tuna steaks *with* mussel *and* white wine sauce

These succulent tuna steaks oven-baked and served with a white wine and mussel sauce make a flavoursome dish. Fresh fish is a good source of protein, B group vitamins and minerals, which are important for healthy brain and nerve function.

ingredients

- 4 tuna steaks, each weighing about 175g (6oz)
- juice of 2 limes
- fresh flatleaf parsley sprigs, to garnish

for the sauce

- 2tbsp cornflour
- 350ml (12fl oz) dry or medium-dry white wine
- 200g (7oz) cooked, shelled mussels (halved, if preferred)
- 15g (½oz) butter
- 3tbsp crème fraîche or light sour cream
- 2tbsp chopped, fresh flatleaf parsley
- sea salt
- freshly ground black pepper

serves *four*
preparation time *10 minutes*
cooking time *20–25 minutes*

method

1 Preheat the oven to 180°C/350°F/gas mark 4.

2 Cut four pieces of non-stick baking paper, each large enough to wrap one tuna steak. Place a tuna steak on each and drizzle over some lime juice. Fold the paper over the fish and twist the edges to secure.

3 Place the parcels on a baking tray and bake for 20–25 minutes, until the fish is cooked and the flesh just flakes when tested with a fork.

4 Meanwhile, make the sauce. In a saucepan, blend the cornflour with a little of the wine. Stir in the remaining wine, then heat gently, stirring constantly, until the sauce comes to the boil and thickens. Simmer gently for 2 minutes, stirring.

5 Stir in the mussels, butter, crème fraîche or light sour cream, parsley and seasoning, and heat gently until piping hot.

6 Open the parcels carefully (to avoid getting burnt by steam) and place the steaks on warmed serving plates. Pour some sauce over each one.

7 Garnish with the parsley sprigs and serve with new potatoes, carrots and celery.

variations

- *Use salmon steaks instead of tuna.*
- *Use lemon juice instead of lime.*
- *Use cooked, peeled prawns instead of mussels.*
- *Use red wine instead of white wine.*

seafood paella

This delicious seafood paella makes a nutritious and substantial meal. Seafood is a good source of protein, B group vitamins and minerals, which support normal brain function.

ingredients

- 1tbsp olive oil
- 1 onion, chopped
- 2 cloves garlic, finely chopped
- 1 red pepper (capsicum), seeded and diced
- 225g (8oz) long grain brown rice
- 225g (8oz) raw, shelled tiger (or king) prawns, plus 4 cooked prawns in their shells, to garnish
- 225g (8oz) prepared raw squid, cut into rings
- large pinch of saffron threads, crushed
- 300ml (½ pint) vegetable stock (see recipe on page 20)
- 300ml (½ pint) dry white wine
- 115g (4oz) fresh or frozen peas
- 3 tomatoes, skinned, seeded and chopped
- sea salt
- freshly ground black pepper
- 225g (8oz) fresh raw mussels in their shells, scrubbed and cleaned
- 2tbsp chopped fresh parsley

serves ***four***
preparation time *15 minutes*
cooking time *45 minutes*

method

1 Heat the oil in a large non-stick frying pan or paella pan. Add the onion, garlic and red pepper, and cook gently for 5 minutes, stirring occasionally.
2 Add the rice, prawns and squid, and cook gently for 5 minutes, stirring occasionally.
3 Stir in the saffron threads, stock, wine, peas, tomatoes and seasoning. Bring to the boil, stirring constantly. Reduce the heat and simmer, uncovered, for about 35 minutes, until most of the stock has been absorbed and the rice is cooked, stirring occasionally.
4 Meanwhile, cook the mussels in a saucepan of boiling water for about 5 minutes, until the shells open. Drain, and discard any mussels that remain closed.
5 Stir the mussels and parsley into the paella and serve immediately, garnished with whole prawns and lemon wedges.
6 Serve with wholemeal bread or a mixed leaf and carrot salad.

variations

- *Use fresh shelled raw scallops instead of the prawns or the squid.*
- *Use mushrooms instead of peas.*
- *Use 2 leeks instead of the onion.*

stir-fried liver *with* mixed greens

When eaten occasionally, tender lamb's liver makes a nutritious dish. Liver is a good source of B group vitamins and iron, both of which are good for normal brain function.

ingredients

- 1tbsp cornflour
- 6tbsp medium-dry cider
- 2tbsp light soy sauce
- 1tbsp wholegrain mustard
- sea salt
- freshly ground black pepper
- 1tbsp olive oil
- 350g (12oz) lamb's liver, cut into thin strips
- 2 leeks, washed and thinly sliced
- 1 red pepper (capsicum), seeded and sliced
- 1 yellow pepper (capsicum), seeded and sliced
- 115g (4oz) spinach, shredded
- 85g (3oz) green (crinkle-leafed) cabbage, shredded
- fresh herb sprigs, to garnish

serves *four*
preparation time *15 minutes*
cooking time *5–7 minutes*

method

1 In a small bowl, blend the cornflour with the cider, then add the soy sauce, mustard and seasoning. Set aside.

2 Heat the oil in a wok or large frying pan. Add the liver and stir-fry over a high heat for 1 minute.

3 Add the leeks, peppers, spinach and cabbage. Stir-fry for 3–4 minutes.

4 Add the cornflour mixture. Stir-fry for 1–2 minutes, until the sauce is thickened and glossy and the liver and vegetables are cooked and tender.

5 Garnish with the herb sprigs and serve with mashed potatoes, carrots and French (green) beans.

variations

- *Use 1 onion instead of the leeks.*
- *Use 1 courgette (zucchini) instead of the yellow pepper.*
- *Use Chinese leaves (greens) instead of cabbage.*

shredded duck *with* ginger *and* lime

Duck breast marinated in lime and ginger and stir-fried with vegetables, makes a delicious, warming meal. Some say ginger is an aid to digestion and helps to lift the mood. Limes are an excellent source of vitamin C.

ingredients

- finely grated rind and juice of 1 lime
- 1tsp ground ginger
- 1tbsp dry sherry
- 1tbsp light soy sauce
- sea salt
- freshly ground black pepper
- 350g (12oz) skinless, boneless duck breast, cut into thin strips
- 1tbsp olive oil
- 1 small fresh red chilli, seeded and finely chopped
- 1 clove garlic, crushed
- 2.5cm (1in) piece of fresh root ginger, peeled and finely chopped
- 1 yellow pepper (capsicum), seeded and sliced
- 6–8 spring onions, chopped
- 175g (6oz) baby sweetcorn
- 115g (4oz) mangetout (snowpeas), trimmed
- toasted sesame seeds, to garnish

serves *four*
preparation time *15 minutes, plus 20 minutes marinating time*
cooking time *8–10 minutes*

method

1 Put the lime rind and juice, ground ginger, sherry, soy sauce and seasoning in a bowl and whisk. Add the duck and toss to mix well. Cover and refrigerate for 20 minutes.

2 Using a slotted spoon, remove the duck from the marinade, and reserve the marinade and duck.

3 Heat the oil in a non-stick wok or large frying pan. Add the chilli, garlic and root ginger, and stir-fry over a high heat for 30 seconds.

4 Add the duck and stir-fry for1–2 minutes until lightly browned.

5 Add the yellow pepper, spring onions, sweetcorn and mangetout, and stir-fry for a further 3–4 minutes.

6 Add the marinade and stir-fry for 2–3 minutes, until the duck is cooked through.

7 Sprinkle with sesame seeds and serve with egg or rice noodles and a mixed dark-green leaf salad.

variations

- *Use sliced mushrooms instead of mangetout (snowpeas).*
- *Use lean chicken, turkey or lamb instead of duck.*
- *Use 1 lemon instead of the lime.*

mediterranean vegetable lasagne

This delicious vegetable lasagne makes a great family meal. The complex carbohydrates found in pasta may help to ease anxiety and irritability and also to revive the body. Vegetables are an excellent source of antioxidants, which can help fight disease.

ingredients

- 1 onion, sliced
- 1 clove garlic, finely chopped
- 1 red pepper (capsicum), seeded and sliced
- 1 yellow pepper (capsicum), seeded and sliced
- 450g (1lb) courgettes (zucchini), sliced
- 350g (12oz) mushrooms, sliced
- 400g (14oz) can tomatoes, chopped
- 227g (8oz) can tomatoes, chopped
- 175g (6oz) quick-cook (instant) lasagne
- 25g (1oz) fresh Parmesan cheese, finely grated
- fresh herb sprigs, to garnish

for the cheese sauce

- 40g (1½oz) butter
- 40g (1½oz) plain wholemeal flour
- ½tsp mustard powder
- 600ml (1 pint) milk
- 115g (4oz) Cheddar cheese, grated
- sea salt
- freshly ground black pepper
- 1–2tbsp chopped, fresh mixed herbs

serves *four to six*
preparation time *25 minutes*
cooking time *45 minutes*

method

1 Preheat the oven to 180°C/350°F/gas mark 4.
2 Put the onion, garlic, peppers, courgettes, mushrooms and tomatoes in a large saucepan. Cover and simmer for 10 minutes, stirring occasionally.
3 Meanwhile, make the cheese sauce. Put the butter, flour, mustard powder and milk in a saucepan and heat gently, whisking continuously, until the sauce comes to the boil and thickens. Simmer gently for 3 minutes.
4 Remove the pan from the heat and stir in the Cheddar cheese, seasoning and herbs.
5 Spoon half the vegetable mixture over the base of a shallow baking tin or ovenproof dish. Cover with half the pasta and top with one-third of the cheese sauce.
6 Repeat these layers, finishing with a layer of cheese sauce. Sprinkle with Parmesan cheese.
8 Bake for about 45 minutes, until cooked and golden brown on top.
9 Garnish with the herb sprigs and serve with wholemeal bread and a mixed dark-green leaf salad.

variations

- *Use 2 leeks instead of the onion.*
- *Use aubergines (eggplants) instead of courgettes.*

freezing instructions

Allow to cool completely, then transfer to a rigid, freezeproof container. Cover, seal and label. Freeze for up to 3 months. Defrost, and reheat in a moderate oven until piping hot.

gnocchi *with* green pesto

Home-made potato gnocchi makes a tasty change from pasta or rice, especially when tossed in a delicious green pesto sauce. Potatoes are a complex carbohydrate, ideal for helping to ease anxiety.

ingredients

for the pesto sauce

- 1 clove garlic, chopped
- 40g (1½oz) fresh basil
- 15g (½oz) fresh parsley
- 55g (2oz) fresh Parmesan cheese, finely grated
- 25g (1oz) pine nuts
- 6tbsp olive oil

for the gnocchi

- 450g (1lb) potatoes, diced
- 225g (8oz) sweet potatoes, diced
- 25g (1oz) fresh Parmesan cheese, finely grated
- 25g (1oz) butter
- 1 medium egg, beaten
- sea salt
- freshly ground black pepper
- 200g (7oz) plain wholemeal flour
- fresh basil sprigs, to garnish

serves *four to six*
preparation time *35 minutes, plus 30 minutes chilling time*
cooking time *20 minutes*

method

1 Blend the pesto ingredients in a food processor.
2 Boil the potatoes for 10–15 minutes, until tender. Drain and mash. Turn into a bowl, add the Parmesan cheese, butter, egg and seasoning, and beat until smooth.
3 Add half the flour, mixing well, then gradually work in the remaining flour, until the dough is smooth, even and slightly sticky. Shape into small balls, place them on a plate and chill for 30 minutes.
4 Cook the gnocchi in batches in lightly salted, simmering water for about 5 minutes, until they float to the surface. Remove using a slotted spoon.
5 Spoon the sauce over the gnocchi, garnish with the basil sprigs and serve with stir-fried mixed vegetables or a salad.

variations

- *Serve the pesto sauce tossed with pasta or baby new potatoes.*
- *Use fresh flatleaf parsley instead of standard parsley.*

chickpea *and* tomato salad

Chickpeas and tomatoes combined with fresh vegetables are tossed in a mildly spiced dressing to make this salad dish. Chickpeas are a good source of B vitamins and zinc, necessary for normal brain function.

ingredients

- 2 x 400g (14oz) cans chickpeas, rinsed and drained
- 350g (12oz) cherry tomatoes, halved
- 115g (4oz) mangetout (snowpeas), chopped
- 1 yellow pepper (capsicum), seeded and diced
- 6–8 spring onions, chopped
- 2tbsp chopped fresh basil
- 2tbsp sunflower or pumpkin seeds (optional)
- fresh basil sprigs, to garnish

for the dressing

- 2tbsp olive oil
- 1tsp ground cumin
- 1tsp ground coriander
- 1tsp hot chilli powder
- 1 clove garlic, crushed
- 175ml (6fl oz) tomato juice
- 2tsp balsamic vinegar
- sea salt
- freshly ground black pepper

serves *four to six*
preparation time *10–15 minutes*
cooking time *2 minutes*

method

1 Put the chickpeas, tomatoes, mangetout, yellow pepper, spring onions, chopped basil and seeds, if using, in a bowl.
2 Heat the oil in a small saucepan, add the ground spices and garlic, and cook gently for 2 minutes, stirring occasionally.
3 Remove the pan from the heat and stir in the tomato juice, balsamic vinegar and seasoning, mixing well.
4 Pour the tomato dressing over the chickpea mixture and toss to mix well. Serve immediately or cool, cover and chill.
5 Garnish with the basil sprigs and serve with wholemeal rolls.

variations

- *Add more ground spices if you like a hotter, spicier flavour.*
- *Use red kidney beans or flageolet beans instead of chickpeas.*
- *Use baby plum (Roma) tomatoes instead of cherry tomatoes.*

fruit *and* nut chocolate slices

These chocolate slices are hard to resist for a special treat. Dried fruit and nuts contain many nutrients, including B vitamins, boron, iron and magnesium, all vital for healthy brain function.

ingredients

- 175g (6oz) plain (dark) chocolate, broken into squares
- 115g (4oz) butter
- 1tbsp maple syrup
- 2tbsp brandy
- 175g (6oz) mixed dried fruit, including sultanas and chopped ready-to-eat dried pineapple, dates, peaches and pears
- 55g (2oz) Brazil nuts, roughly chopped
- 55g (2oz) cashew nuts, halved

makes *24 small bars or squares*
preparation time *15 minutes, plus chilling time*

method

1 Lightly grease and line an 18cm (7in) square cake tin.
2 Put the chocolate, butter and syrup in a medium-sized bowl over a saucepan of simmering water and stir until melted.
3 Remove the bowl from the pan and beat the brandy into the chocolate mixture.
4 Stir in the dried fruits and nuts. Transfer the mixture to the tin and smooth to level the surface. Set aside to cool, then chill in the refrigerator until firm.
5 Cut into small bars or squares and serve on their own or with fresh fruit, such as strawberries and kiwifruit, for a delicious dessert.

variations

- *Use honey instead of maple syrup.*
- *Use whisky instead of brandy.*
- *Use chopped almonds and hazelnuts instead of Brazil nuts and cashew nuts.*

fruit *with* strawberry coulis

A platter of fresh fruit served with a strawberry coulis makes a wonderful dessert. Fresh fruit is a rich source of vitamin C, which the body needs in greater amounts when under stress.

ingredients

- 1 small mango
- 2 apricots
- 1 kiwifruit
- 2 papaya (or 1 medium-sized paw paw)
- 4 fresh figs
- 115g (4oz) large, ripe blackberries
- fresh mint sprigs, to decorate

for the coulis

- 225g (8oz) strawberries
- 1tbsp honey
- 1–2tsp cherry brandy or apple liqueur

serves *four*
preparation time *20 minutes*

method

1 Put the strawberries in a blender or food processor and blend until smooth. Press the strawberry purée through a sieve and discard the seeds.
2 Pour the purée into a bowl, add the honey and cherry brandy or liqueur and mix well. Cover and set aside.
3 Peel, stone and slice the mango. Halve and stone the apricots, and peel and quarter the kiwifruit. Peel, seed and slice the papaya and quarter the figs.
4 Arrange the fresh fruit on a large serving platter, decorate with the mint sprigs and serve with the strawberry coulis served separately in a jug alongside. Drizzle the coulis over individual servings of fruit.

variations

- *Use fresh ripe raspberries or blackberries instead of strawberries.*
- *Choose your own selection of fruit to serve on the platter.*

apricot upside-down pudding

This family favourite is delicious served with a little crème fraîche, light sour cream or home-made custard. Fresh, canned and dried apricots contain many of the vitamins and minerals that are necessary for a healthy brain and nervous system.

ingredients

- 4tbsp maple syrup
- 175g (6oz) ready-to-eat dried apricots, chopped
- 220g (8oz) can apricots in fruit juice, drained and chopped
- 115g (4oz) butter
- 115g (4oz) light brown sugar
- 2 medium eggs, beaten
- 175g (6oz) plain wholemeal flour
- 1tsp baking powder
- 1tsp ground cinnamon
- about 3tbsp milk

serves *four to six*
preparation time *20 minutes*
cooking time *45 minutes*

method

1 Preheat the oven to 180°C/350°F/gas mark 4.

2 Lightly grease and line a deep, 18cm (7in) round cake tin. Spoon or pour the maple syrup over the base.

3 Mix the dried and canned apricots and scatter them evenly over the syrup. Set the tin aside.

4 Cream the butter and sugar in a bowl until pale and fluffy. Add the eggs gradually, beating well after each addition.

5 Fold in the flour, baking powder and cinnamon, adding enough milk to make a soft, dropping consistency. Spread the mixture evenly over the apricots and level the surface.

6 Bake for about 45 minutes, until the sponge has risen and is springy to the touch and golden brown.

7 Turn out onto a serving plate and serve hot or cold in wedges, with a little crème fraîche, light sour cream or home-made custard.

variations

- *Use dried and canned pears or peaches instead of apricots.*
- *Use honey instead of maple syrup.*
- *Use ground ginger or mixed spice instead of cinnamon.*

freezing instructions

Allow to cool completely, then wrap in foil, seal and label. Freeze for up to 3 months. Defrost for several hours at room temperature. Reheat in a moderate oven until piping hot.

it's been a hard day's night

FLAGGING AFTER A HARD *day? You need a quick fix of calming nutrients and comforting foods that can help you unwind and disperse the feelings of tension – so tuck into this delicious and nutritious menu from the reviving foods section for a dose of nutritional therapy.*

green bean vinaigrette

Green beans contain calcium, magnesium and vitamin C.

ingredients

- 700g (1lb 9oz) French (green) beans, trimmed
- 150ml (¼ pint) French dressing (see recipe on page 21)
- 55g (2oz) flaked almonds, toasted

serves *six*
preparation time *10 minutes*
cooking time *5–6 minutes*

method

1 Cook the beans in lightly salted, boiling water for 5–6 minutes, until cooked and tender but still crisp. Drain well.
2 Serve the beans hot or cold, with the French dressing drizzled over the top. Sprinkle with the flaked almonds just before serving.
3 Serve with crusty wholemeal bread or rolls.

mediterranean vegetable lasagne

The complex carbohydrates in the pasta and vitamin C-rich vegetables are great stress relievers.

ingredients

- 1 onion, sliced
- 1 clove garlic, finely chopped
- 1 red pepper (capsicum), seeded and sliced
- 1 yellow pepper (capsicum), seeded and sliced
- 450g (1lb) courgettes (zucchini), sliced
- 350g (12oz) mushrooms, sliced
- 400g (14oz) can tomatoes, chopped
- 227g (8oz) can tomatoes, chopped
- 175g (6oz) quick-cook (instant) lasagne
- 25g (1oz) fresh Parmesan cheese, finely grated
- fresh herb sprigs, to garnish

for the cheese sauce

- 40g (1½oz) butter
- 40g (1½oz) plain wholemeal flour
- ½tsp mustard powder
- 600ml (1 pint) milk
- 115g (4oz) Cheddar cheese, grated
- sea salt
- freshly ground black pepper
- 1–2tbsp chopped, fresh mixed herbs

serves *four to six*
preparation time *25 minutes*
cooking time *45 minutes*

method

1 Preheat the oven to 180°C/350°F/gas mark 4.
2 Put the onion, garlic, peppers, courgettes, mushrooms and tomatoes in a large saucepan. Cover and simmer for 10 minutes, stirring occasionally.
3 Meanwhile, make the cheese sauce. Put the butter, flour, mustard powder and milk in a saucepan and heat gently, whisking continuously, until the sauce comes to the boil and thickens. Simmer gently for 3 minutes.
4 Remove the pan from the heat and stir in the Cheddar cheese, seasoning and herbs.
5 Spoon half the vegetable mixture over the base of a shallow baking tin or ovenproof dish. Cover with half the pasta and top with one-third of the cheese sauce.
6 Repeat these layers, finishing with a layer of cheese sauce. Sprinkle with Parmesan cheese.
8 Bake for about 45 minutes, until cooked and golden brown on top.
9 Garnish with the herb sprigs and serve with wholemeal bread and a mixed dark-green leaf salad.

apricot upside-down pudding

This warm, fruity, cake-like pudding is a comforting way to round off this soothing menu.

ingredients

- 4tbsp maple syrup
- 175g (6oz) ready-to-eat dried apricots, chopped
- 220g (8oz) can apricots in fruit juice, drained and chopped
- 115g (4oz) butter
- 115g (4oz) light brown sugar
- 2 medium eggs, beaten
- 175g (6oz) plain wholemeal flour
- 1tsp baking powder
- 1tsp ground cinnamon
- about 3tbsp milk

serves *four to six*
preparation time *20 minutes*
cooking time *45 minutes*

method

1 Preheat the oven to 180°C/350°F/gas mark 4.
2 Lightly grease and line a deep, 18cm (7in) round cake tin. Spoon or pour the maple syrup over the base.
3 Mix the dried and canned apricots and scatter them evenly over the syrup. Set the tin aside.
4 Cream the butter and sugar in a bowl until pale and fluffy. Add the eggs gradually, beating well after each addition.
5 Fold in the flour, baking powder and cinnamon, adding enough milk to make a soft, dropping consistency. Spread the mixture evenly over the apricots and level the surface.
6 Bake for about 45 minutes, until the sponge has risen and is springy to the touch and golden brown.
7 Turn out onto a serving plate and serve hot or cold in wedges, with some crème fraîche, light sour cream or home-made custard.

which mind problem *needs which* food?

poor sleep and insomnia

- Poor sleep can result from eating meals that are high in protein late at night. Protein foods, such as eggs, cheese, meat and poultry, stimulate the mind and keep you awake. Complex carbohydrates, such as cereals, rice and pasta, may help calm an overactive mind. A small bowl of muesli or oat-based cereal eaten about an hour before bedtime can encourage sounder sleep.
- Insomnia is often a symptom of depression or stress, so while proper nutrition can help, it is also important to identify the root cause of any anxiety.

premenstrual syndrome (PMS)

- Premenstrual syndrome may be related to a woman's changing hormone levels. To help with irritability, depression and lethargy, as well as the other physical symptoms of PMS, such as bloating and tender breasts, some nutritionists recommend increasing the intake of foods that contain useful amounts of B_6, such as meat, poultry, fish, wheatgerm, cantaloupe (orange-fleshed) melon, and green leafy vegetables. Research has shown that women who avoid sugar and caffeine and take regular exercise may experience a significant reduction in PMS.

problem

which mood problem *needs which* food?

stress

• When you are under stress, your body uses more vitamin C, which is vital for the production of the hormone noradrenalin, from the adrenal glands. Increase your intake of vitamin C by eating plenty of fresh fruit and vegetables, at least five portions a day. Top sources include oranges, grapefruit, kiwifruit, lemons, peppers (capsicums), tomatoes and green leafy vegetables.

mood swings

• Mood swings, nervousness, anxiety, irritability and apathy can result from a deficiency of B group vitamins, which are essential to proper brain function. As all B group vitamins work closely with each other, it is important to include them together in the diet. To get the widest range of B group vitamins, include as many as possible of the following: apricots, avocado, bananas, melon, dried fruits, nuts, seeds dark-green leafy vegetables, root vegetables, pulses, brown rice, oats, eggs and poultry, lean meats, seafood, and yoghurt and other dairy products.

vitamins *and* minerals

FOODS CONTAIN DIFFERENT amounts of nutrients, and no single food can provide all the nutrients needed for good health. Vitamins and minerals found in foods work synergistically with proteins, carbohydrates, fats and each other. To make sure you obtain sufficient nutrients, vary your diet as much as possible. The following lists are a guide to recommended daily nutritional requirements.

Fat-soluble vitamins

vitamin A

from retinol in animal products and beta carotene in plant foods

Vital for growth and cell development, vision and immune function. Maintains healthy skin, hair, nails, bones and teeth.

vitamin D

calciferols

Needed for calcium absorption; helps build and maintain strong bones and teeth.

vitamin E

tocopherols

Protects fatty acids; maintains muscles and red blood cells; a major antioxidant.

vitamin K

phylloquinone, menaquinone

Essential for proper blood clotting.

Water-soluble vitamins

biotin

Needed to release energy from food. Important in the synthesis of fat and cholesterol.

folate

folic acid, folacin

Required for cell division and the formation of DNA, RNA and proteins in the body. Extra needed before conception and in pregnancy to protect against neural tube defects.

vitamin B_1

thiamin

Needed to obtain energy from carbohydrates, fats and alcohol; prevents the build-up of toxins in the body that may damage the heart and nervous system.

vitamin B_2

riboflavin

Needed to release energy from food and to assist the functioning of vitamin B_6 and niacin.

vitamin B_3

niacin, nicotine acid, nicotinamide

Needed to produce energy in cells. Helps to maintain healthy skin and an efficient digestive system.

vitamin B_5

pantothenic acid

Helps to release energy from food. Essential to the synthesis of cholesterol, fat and red blood cells.

vitamin B_6

pyridoxine, pyridoxamine, pyridoxal

Helps to release energy from proteins; important for immune function, the nervous system and the formation of red blood cells.

vitamin B_{12}

cyanocobalamin

Needed to make red blood cells, DNA, RNA and myelin (for nerve fibres).

vitamin C

ascorbic acid

Vitamin C is a major antioxidant, vital for healthy immune function, and for the production of collagen (a protein essential for healthy gums, teeth, bones, cartilage and skin). It also aids the absorption of iron from plant food.

Minerals

calcium

Builds strong bones and teeth; vital to muscle and nerve function and blood clotting.

chloride

Maintains proper body chemistry. Used to make digestive juices.

chromium

Helps to regulate blood sugar levels and blood cholesterol levels.

copper

Needed for bone growth and connective tissue formation. It helps the body to absorb iron from food and is present in many enzymes that protect against free radicals.

iodine

Necessary for the manufacture of thyroid hormones.

iron

Needed for the manufacture of red blood cells and for energy production within cells.

magnesium

Stimulates bone growth, assists in nerve impulses, and is important for muscle contraction.

manganese

Vital component of various enzymes involved in energy production; helps to form bone and connective tissue.

molybdenum

Essential component of enzymes involved in the production of DNA and RNA; may fight tooth decay.

potassium

Helps to regulate the body's fluid balance and distribution, to keep the heartbeat regular and maintain normal blood pressure. It is important for muscle and nerve function.

phosphorus

Helps maintain strong bones and teeth. However, in excess (such as results from excessive consumption of fizzy drinks) it adversely affects the body's ability to use calcium and magnesium.

selenium

A major antioxidant that works with vitamin E to protect cell membranes from damage due to oxidation.

sodium

Works with potassium to regulate the body's fluid balance; essential for proper nerve and muscle function.

sulphur

Component of two essential amino acids that help to form many proteins in the body.

zinc

Essential for normal growth, reproduction and immune function.

vitamins

	UK		AUSTRALIA AND NEW ZEALAND		SOUTH AFRICA	
	Daily Requirement†		Recommended Dietary Intakes†		Recommended Daily Allowances†	
	MEN	**WOMEN**	**MEN**	**WOMEN**	**MEN**	**WOMEN**
Vitamin A	700mcg	600mcg (950mcg in lactation)	750mcg.	750mcg (1200mcg in lactation)	1000mg	800mg (1300mg in lactation)
Vitamin D	Enough vitamin D is made when the skin is exposed to sunlight. People who are confined indoors require about 10 mcg from the diet.					
Vitamin E	At least 4mg	At least 3mg	10mg	7mg	10mg	8mg
Vitamin K	70mcg	65mcg	– *	– *	70–80mcg	60–65mcg
Biotin	10–200mcg	10–200mcg	– *	– *	30–100mcg	30–100mcg
Folate	200mcg	200mcg (400mcg in pregnancy)	200mcg	200mcg (400mcg in pregnancy; 350 mcg in lactation)	200mcg	180mcg (400mcg in pregnancy)
Vitamin B_1 (Thiamin)	1mg	0.8mg	1.1mg	0.8mg	1.5mg	1.1mg
Vitamin B_2 (Riboflavin)	1.3mg	1.1mg	1.7mg	1.2mg	1.7mg	1.3mg
Vitamin B_3 (Niacin)	17mg	13mg	19mg	13mg	19mg	15mg
Vitamin B_5 (Pantothenic acid)	3–7mg	3–7mg	– *	– *	4–7mg	4–7mg
Vitamin B_6 (Pyridoxine)	1.4mg	1.2mg	1.3–1.9mg	0.9–1.4mg	2.0mg	1.6mg
Vitamin B_{12} (cyanocobalamin)	1.5mcg	1.5mcg	2mcg	2mcg	2.0mcg	2.0mcg
Vitamin C	40mg (smokers at least 80mg)	40mg	40mg (smokers at least 80mg)	30mg	60mg (smokers at least 80–120mg)	60mg

† *Pregnant and lactating women require a slightly higher intake of most vitamins, and should be guided by their doctor or nutritionist.*

* *No daily requirement established.*

minerals

	UK		AUSTRALIA AND NEW ZEALAND		SOUTH AFRICA	
	Daily Requirement†		Recommended Dietary Intakes†		Recommended Daily Allowances†	
	MEN	**WOMEN**	**MEN**	**WOMEN**	**MEN**	**WOMEN**
Calcium	700mg	700mg	800mg	800mg (1000mg after menopause)	800mg	800mg
Chloride	2500mg	2500mg	– *	– *	750mg	750mg
Chromium	25mcg	25mcg	– *	– *	50–200mcg	50–200mcg
Copper	1.2mg	1.2mg	– *	– *	1.5–3.0mg	1.5–3.0mg
Iodine	140mcg	140mcg	150mcg	120mcg	150mcg	150mcg
Iron	8.7mg	14. 5mg	7mg	12–16mg (5–7mg after menopause)	10mg	15mg
Magnesium	300mg	270mg	320mg	270mg	350mg	280mg
Manganese	1.4mg	1.4mg	– *	– *	2.0–5.0mg	2.0–5.0mg
Molybdenum	50–400mcg	50–400mcg	– *	– *	75–250mcg	75–250mcg
Phosphorus	550mg	550mg	1000mg	1000mg	800mg	800mg
Potassium	3500mg	3500mg	50–140mmol	50–140mmol	2000mg	2000mg
Selenium	75mcg	60mcg	85mcg	70mcg	70mcg	55mcg
Sodium	1600mg	1600mg	40–100mmol	40–100mmol	500mg	500mg
Sulphur	There is no set dietary requirement in any of these countries					
Zinc	9.5mg	7mg	12mg	12mg	15mg	12mg

† *Pregnant and lactating women require a slightly higher intake of most vitamins, and should be guided by their doctor or nutritionist.*

* *No daily requirement established.*

index

acknowledgements

Grateful thanks to my colleague Dr John Briffa for his advice with this book and to my co-author Kathryn Marsden for being a true friend.

Hazel Courteney

Many people have worked very hard to prepare this book. My respect and admiration must go, in particular, to Hazel Courteney, and to Anne Sheasby who created the sumptuous store of recipes. It has been a pleasure to work with such conscientious and caring professionals.

Kathryn Marsden

I would like to thank Robert for his on-going support and encouragement with this book and for his tireless tasting of all the recipes; Kathryn Marsden for all her help and advice; Anne Townley and Viv Croot for asking me to create all the recipes for this book; and Molly Perham and Caroline Earle for all their hard editing work.

Anne Sheasby